A Memoir in Pieces

Books by Ernest Hillen

The Way of a Boy: A Memoir of Java

Small Mercies: A Boy after War

A Weekend Memoir

A Memoir in Pieces

A Memoir in Pieces

Ernest Hillen

Rock's Mills Press
Oakville, Ontario
2017

Published by
ROCK'S MILLS PRESS
www.rocksmillspress.com

Cover photos: Hillen with sword (Denis Plain, *Perspectives Dimanches*); old man (Ernest Hillen, *Weekend*), Don Messer (B. Brooks, National Film Board, LAC Mikan no. 3211990), Allanah Myles (Rob Doda, Wikimedia Commons).

Library and Archives Canada (LAC) Cataloguing in Publication data is available from the publisher. For this and other inquiries, contact us at customer.service@rocksmillspress.com.

For Marta and Maia

Contents

Introduction

Nothing human is alien to me.

Those words, from the playwright Terence of Rome (b. 185 BC, more or less) make a point about the journalist Ernest Hillen: nothing human was alien to him. He was just as curious about the storekeeper, the refugee, or the pop star as he was about the stone-cold Canadian mercenary soldier.

He knew that they are us.

And so he did what the best writers have always done, from the beginning of time: he gave us the facts of the human condition—the sights, the sounds, the smells of life—and trusted that his readers were smart enough to draw their own conclusions about who we are on this glorious and miserable planet.

Ernest Hillen is one of the finest journalists this country has produced, and he was at the height of his powers at a time which coincided with the flowering of New Journalism in the United States, and the rise of cultural nationalism in Canada—the years bracketing the Centennial, when we were concerned with what it was like to live here, and equally concerned with what the world looked like through Canadian eyes.

For those of us who grew up in small towns a long time ago, *Weekend Magazine*, where most of these pieces first appeared, was our national microscope and our international telescope.

The appetite for a Hillen story in those days was large but if, in the end, there are really only a very few stories—we are born, we die, we do things, and things are done to us—then what differentiates between them is detail, and here is where Hillen shines:

When he tells us that a Saturday lunch at the home of the actor Bob Homme consisted of hamburgers, pickles, tea and Scotch, we learn as much about the Friendly Giant as we do about the man who played him on CBC Television.

When he tells us that the cantankerous west coast talk show host, Jack Webster, drank fifteen cups of coffee and fired up five packs of cigarettes a day, then you know it is not just an accurate account of one man's appetites, but an explanation of the Webster growl without the need to say so directly.

More grimly, when we learn that the Montreal high school kid who became a soldier for hire in Africa vomited the first time he saw a tangle of severed human limbs rotting on a jungle riverbank, that single detail tells us something crucial about the man who overcame a revulsion of death and learned himself to kill and leave bodies behind.

In all these instances, our reactions to a Hillen story tell us something about ourselves.

If you have read well and widely enough, you will already be familiar with *The Way of a Boy*, Hillen's brilliant memoir about growing up in Indonesia. Those years included the years spent with his mother in a Japanese internment camp during the Second World War, and that book is as close to perfection as any memoir I have read.

A couple of those Indonesia pieces bracket this wide-ranging and invaluable collection, and having read them and re-read them, I'm now going to take a stab at something I think is important:

I venture that Hillen's childhood experiences are what made him a journalist. Because I think that a boy, imprisoned with his mother, learns at least two things:

The first is how to pay close attention, because when punishment is cruel and capricious, a boy will learn to watch for signs of, and to be always aware of, the triggers of provocation; in other words, he learns deep observation as a way of life.

The second lesson is how not to be noticed, so as not to stand out or otherwise attract the sort of attention which might then lead to punishment.

Those two things—close watching, and a kind of practical invisibility—are, when combined with natural curiosity, the keys to the writer's craft.

In Hillen's case, there is one more thing. English is not his first language—he grew up speaking Dutch, and did not learn English until later in life.

So I would make the obvious comparisons to other writers—Conrad, Brodsky, Nabokov, Achebe—and say that his art, like theirs, was the ability to tell the most complex stories using a second language, one that is deceptively simple and all the better for it.

Hillen is very much a man of his time, and had his own circumstances been different he might not have become a journalist. He might have been a caretaker in a school in Holland, or held any number of jobs, although mercenary is not one of them—there isn't a hurtful bone in his body; and anyone who knows him smiles fondly at the mention of his name. Not always true of journalists.

Among his peers, colleagues and contemporaries is the journalist and veteran CBC Radio host Michael Enright. When asked where he would place Hillen in the pantheon of the feature writer, Enright cited *The New Yorker* magazine and observed that, if founding editor Harold Ross had had the chance, he would have hired Ernest third. If that's elliptical, I would simply say that it puts Hillen on a par with Janet Flanner, or E.B. White.

Except for one thing.

He is ours.

JOE FIORITO

Preface

"Pieces," of course, is a word journalists use a lot because putting together pieces is what they do—articles, reports, features, profiles, interviews, columns, and so on. This selection spans my years writing for Canadian magazines, with gaps when I was working with words, but not selling them, and when I was travelling or living abroad. Hence, *A Memoir in Pieces*. The culling was based on my real liking for these stories and their diversity. (A clutch of them, after all, led to writing two books!)

Thanks are due to the fascinating people I've been privileged to meet, in Canada and beyond, who, with such grace, permitted me to listen, observe, question, and participate a little in their lives. It was easy to grow fond of many and so, like a pirate, I carried away not only their stories but also those rich affections. The debt stands.

There are five editors I've owed a good deal over the years, including friendship: Peter Hendry (*The Family Herald*), Paul Rush (*Weekend Magazine* and *The Financial Post Magazine*), Kevin Doyle (*Maclean's*), Peter Worthington (*Influence Magazine*), and John Fraser (*Saturday Night*).

And, to the present, I'd like to thank the imaginative David Stover, editor and publisher of Rock's Mills Press who had the fine perspicacity to reach out to bring these stories to a new audience. In 2009, as president of Oxford University Press Canada, he did the same thing when he issued the first collection, *A Weekend Memoir*.

As always, my wife Marta Tomins is both in-house editor and my life's joy.

ERNEST HILLEN

Credits

The articles included in this book originally appeared in the following publications:

"Japanese Prison Camp: 1944, Java," *Weekend Magazine*, December 21, 1968; **"Always on a Thursday,"** *Family Herald*, April 13, 1967; **"Killing is His Business,"** *Weekend Magazine*, February 8, 1969; **"The Friendliest Giant,"** *Weekend Magazine*, April 19, 1969; **"The Death of *Don Messer's Jubilee*,"** *Weekend Magazine*, June 21, 1969; **"The Man They Love To Hate,"** *Weekend Magazine*, February 6, 1971; **"Path to Yesterday,"** *Weekend Magazine*, May 15, 1971; **"The Hottest Hot-liner of Them All,"** *Weekend Magazine*, June 19, 1971; **"So Many Will Die,"** *Weekend Magazine*, July 31, 1971; **"Ninety Seconds of Daylight,"** *Weekend Magazine*, December 4, 1971; **"Biafra: A Time To Heal,"** *Weekend Magazine*, September 30, 1972; **"Banana, Glue, Rubber Face, and Eight Other Canadians: The Men Behind Sonny and Cher,"** *Weekend Magazine*, March 10, 1973; **"My Aquarium Is Not So Much a Place for Fish as for People,"** *Weekend Magazine*, September 8, 1973; **"'Bitaemo' to the Town of Dauphin, Manitoba,"** *Weekend Magazine*, September 22, 1973; **"Learning the Ropes,"** *Weekend Magazine*, September 29, 1973; **"Samurai Swordsman,"** published in French in *Perspectives Dimanches,* July 24, 1977; **"The Good Life in a Good Place,"** *The Financial Post Magazine*, April 14, 1979; **"Explorer-Poet of the Last Frontier,"** *Maclean's*, March 10, 1980; **"The Little Shop on Main Street,"** *The Financial Post Magazine*, July/August, 1981; **"Three-Piece Perfection,"** *The Financial Post Magazine*, May 1, 1982; **"Going Out in Style,"** *The Financial Post Moneywise Magazine*, December 1986; **"Myles To Go,"** *Saturday Night*, November 1991; **"The Tyrant's Touch,"** *The Wall Street Journal*, August 28, 1990; **"My Wound,"** *The Idler*, July/August, 1989; **"Hubie and I,"** *Saturday Night*, December 1990; **"Back on Java,"** *Saturday Night*, July/August, 1990. **"Reporting a War's Aftermath"** has not hitherto been published. The author and publisher acknowledge the kind assistance of Postmedia in allowing the reprinting of material originally appearing in magazines published by its predecessor companies, including *Weekend Magazine, The Family Herald, Perspectives Dimanches, The Financial Post Magazine*, and *The Financial Post Moneywise Magazine*.

A Memoir in Pieces

1. Japanese Prison Camp: 1944, Java (1968)

It's night, and we lie waiting for the sound of the "tokkeh" up in the bamboo rafters. A tokkeh is a lizard with large bulging eyes, and four toes on each foot. When it grows dark and there's one in the barrack, you wait for it to clear its throat, just like a human being, and go "tokkeh, tokkeh." If it "tokkehs" seven times it means good luck.

It's only just past eight. At eight exactly, every night, the two light bulbs in the barrack go out. You stop talking then; everybody does, in all the barracks in the camp. The adults—women—always tell us that's because you have to save your strength. Tomorrow is another day in the gardens with water only at noon. So save your strength, go to sleep.

But this is a different night. It's Christmas. I can hear people still talking softly in the dark, even laughing. There are about 200 women and children in our barrack.

She is lying next to me under half a bed sheet; I have the other half. It's so hot, you don't really need any covering but it keeps off the mosquitoes and if you sweat you tuck it between your legs so they don't stick. We lie on bamboo mats spread over the bamboo slats that make up our bed. The bed stretches the length of the barrack and across from us separated by an earthen path is another bed. Each person has a space measuring two by five feet. You eat there, sleep there, you lie there when you're sick, and you keep your clothes, spoons, cups and mugs there. She and I also have a fork, and a tin can with a top which has four tablespoons of sugar we've saved up.

She lies on her back in the dark with her hands under her head and her sheet doesn't cover her legs. Mine does, I can even get my head under it.

The day begins a little before six when a bell calls us out to stand in front of the barrack to be counted by the soldiers. We stand in rows of six and bow deeply when they walk by. Those of us in front count loud and very fast in Japanese: "*Ichi-ni-san-si-go-roku-hichi . . .*" She has *hichi,* seven, and you say it like a sneeze, "Hi-chiiii!"

Then to work in the vegetable gardens—outside. At noon we drink water from gasoline cans which women have carried to us strung by wire from bamboo poles on their necks. I don't see her 'til evening. I work in the garden where all the boys work. I am nine and one of the biggest.

By six we're back inside, in front of the barrack, and counted again. Then everybody bathes in the bathing and toilet barrack. There are eight big barrels of water and you take a margarine can with a handle inside, dip it in the barrel and splash yourself. There's no soap. The toilet is a narrow ditch with running water over which you squat. She asks me to try and go when it gets dark because I'm one of the biggest boys and I shouldn't be bathing and going to the bathroom with women. So I splash myself, alone, without taking off the shorts I've had on all day.

Today was special because it was Christmas. They promised three things for the evening meal: Double bread, soup with meat, and half a hard-boiled egg per person. We hadn't had egg for a long time. I thought as often of eating egg as of eating cold fruit salad. Sometimes I told her that the first thing I wanted when we were free would be eggs and cold fruit salad. We discussed the different kinds of fruit we would cut up above a bowl to catch the juice. Eggs we would eat in just a few bites because there would be lots of them. Now when we get an egg she takes our fork and mashes it and we eat it slowly. That way, she explains, you get *all* the goodness.

From the camp kitchen we took the bread, the soup and the egg back to the barrack. We ate on our bed, saving the egg for last.

She wore her long red hair in two braids wrapped around the back of her head. When we were done with the bread and the soup, she looked at me and said:

"Erik was put in the hospital this morning."

Erik was three. He was the youngest child of a friend of hers who lived a few barracks away and whom I called Aunt.

"Erik is very sick. He has dysentery."

Dysentery meant you had to go to the bathroom all the time. If you caught it, you often died. But I would have liked her now to start peeling the egg and mashing it.

"I think we should give half our egg to Aunt to give to Erik. We can do that because we are both still strong, and we'll have the other half between us."

I didn't know what to say. She never said silly things but this seemed silly. For one thing, Aunt never mashed the eggs for her children. They just ate theirs in a few bites.

"Erik may die, you know."

I still thought it was silly. You didn't *give* things away; you traded, for other things. Anyhow, half an egg wouldn't make Erik better. He wasn't a strong boy, and he never got brown in the sun, just red.

"It may not help Erik get better, but we should try . . . ."

She paused.

"I think your brother would have said yes."

That was true, Jerry probably would have. He had been taken away the year before when he was 12. All boys of 12 and over, they said, were a danger to the state. We didn't know where he was.

So, in the end, we gave the half egg to Aunt . . . who probably let Erik just gulp it down.

Our own half she mashed with the fork, then divided it into two neat piles which we ate slowly. Then she gave herself a spoonful of sugar from the tin can and me a spoon and a half because, she said, I was a child and at Christmas children should always be given more than adults. We ate the sugar slowly, too.

In a little while it was eight o'clock and the light bulbs went out. She lay next to me under her sheet that didn't cover her legs, and I knew her long red hair was not in braids now but lying loose about her head. As a small boy, about as old as Erik, when I had been a very good son, she had let me brush it.

People went on talking softly and sometimes laughing even though they should save their strength. But it didn't go on for very long. It became quiet, and I knew that they, like me, were waiting for the tokkeh to scrape its throat.

2. Always on a Thursday (1967)

VALENCIA, SPAIN—Are farmers always the best judges of farmers' problems? According to perhaps the oldest continuous court of law in the world—yes.

Every Thursday noon in a small, fenced-off space in the shadow of the Cathedral of Valencia, Spain, the Country Irrigation Court of Valencia goes into session—as it has done every Thursday for 1,000 years. The unique little tribunal is presided over by farmers, its rules have been devised by farmers, and it is farmers who come there as the accusers and the accused.

As a historic sight, it is not very impressive. It is old in a shabby, neglected way. The sculpture work on the Cathedral's Apostles' Gate, under which the Court sits, is scratched and chipped, the human figures maimed, the stone blackened with soot. The wrought-iron fence is worn smooth from people leaning against it; its gate, hung on wobbly hinges, is held shut with a big, rusty lock. Eight dusty, straight-backed chairs sit in a half circle inside the fence. The seating of three of them is ripped. Each chair carries a nameplate for one of the main canals that water the Province of Valencia: Quart, Mestalla, Tor Mas . . . .

Spaniards themselves admit they are not a very punctual people. But two things, they say, always start on time—the bullfight and the Country Irrigation Court of Valencia. Yet at 11:53, seven minutes to Court time, not a soul on the sidewalk by the church appears the least concerned. A moment later, though, like actors running on stage before curtains, people are making for the spot from all directions. Tires screech. A streetcar jerks to a halt. People bump into each other. The eight old chairs seem to take on life as they become the centre of things. By 11:55 there is a crowd two-deep around the fence. By 11:57 it is five-deep. At 11:58 an old man wearing a chauffeur's cap, a short black gown, and carrying a rusty pike, pushes his way through the people and unlocks the gate. He is the Peace Officer of the Court. Now the eight judges, aged between 50 and 60, file into the tiny arena and take their seats. They wear long black gowns, but no caps. Their faces are leathery, lined, and burned by the sun. The Peace Officer faces the centre chair, where the President sits, and lifting his cap, asks in a loud voice if proceedings may begin. It is exactly 12 o'clock.

On a nod from the President, the Peace Officer turns to the crowd and shouts: "The accused of the Canal of Quart!" If there is an accused, and if there are plaintiffs, they are now to come forward. If not, he shouts the same for the next canal, and so on, ending with the eighth, Robella.

Formed in 960 during the Moorish occupation of Spain, the Court was left intact when in 1238 the area was freed of Mohammedan rule. Successive

Christian rulers, while scrapping much of their predecessors' legislation, recognized the simple, practical way in which the Court dispensed justice in regard to the distribution of irrigation water, and left it alone.

Speaking slowly in English, Señor Vicente Giner Boira, the Court's legal consultant for 25 years, said: "It is not presumptuous to say that the Court stands today as a monument to the good sense and the common sense of farmers throughout history." Mr. Giner's father had the job before him for 50 years; his grandfather for 30. "Very little has been changed in either the laws or the procedure of the Court over the centuries," he said.

"The rules, or statutes, of the Court are the most important legislation ever exported by Spain. They are applied, for instance, in all South American countries today. Yet it is so simple: the laws are made of the customs of the people—these are practical and, therefore, popular."

He explained how it worked.

The River Turia is the largest river in the province. The eight canals which traverse the so-called orchard of Valencia (where the finest Spanish oranges are produced) feed from it and allow even the last field in the area to get the water it needs. Farmers who benefit from the water of a particular canal are the common proprietors of that water and each, in proportion to the land he owns, has the right to the amount his land needs. The water is thus an integral part of the land; whoever sells a piece of his land also sells the right to irrigate and the water of which he is part-owner.

Connecting with each of the "mother canals" is a network of smaller ones. Farmers living within this network form a "community of irrigators" which governs distribution of the water. The communities are ruled by statutes which were passed on orally by the Arabs, and no one thought to write into law until early in the 18th century. Seeing to their observance is a committee whose membership is changed every three years. Its head, or trustee, is elected by popular vote from among the community's farmers. To qualify he must be "an honest worker of good fame" and own enough land, on which he must work himself, to make a decent living. Absentee landowners and day laborers are not eligible. Besides assuming executive power over the canal community, the trustee also becomes one of the Irrigation Court's eight judges.

One instance of how simply the tribunal operates is that when the accused does not appear after being summoned on three consecutive Thursdays, his case is handled in his absence and he is, almost automatically, found guilty and penalized. Mr. Giner said this system works very well. The police have never yet been asked for help.

Denunciations are usually made for these reasons: stealing water; damaging wall-boundaries (between farms); deviating water—directing it, for instance, to a nearby field already irrigated and damaging a crop through an excess of water; not keeping a canal clean so water can flow through freely; lifting the sluice gate when it's another's turn, causing him to miss it and waste water; and irrigating without having asked permission for one's turn.

To insure impartiality, the trustee to whose canal administration the quarrelling parties belong cannot take part in discussion of the case. Also, if the accused belongs to a canal community on the right side of the river, only the trustees of the canals on the left side will pronounce judgement, and vice versa. Proceedings are entirely oral (in the Valencian dialect which is only spoken in the countryside) and nothing is ever written down. Sentences are without appeal.

The little court's authority and the esteem in which it is held by irrigators sometimes surpasses that of the Supreme Court of Spain, said Mr. Giner. Perhaps because even the trustees are not safe from it. They, too, are irrigators, after all.

Recently, it was the President himself who was denounced. One of his day laborers, it seemed, had committed some infringement. On the following Thursday, the watchman of the canal of which the President is the trustee presented his denunciation. The President had no choice but to get up and take his place where the accused stands. Questioned by his colleagues he was found guilty. The Court's Vice-President then pronounced the usual formula—"This court condemns you to pay the penalty and the costs according to the statutes"—whereupon he could sit down in his own chair again, and the next case was called.

By 12:08, on many a Thursday, it's all over, and the crowd is soon dispersed. The Court rarely has much business; actually all concerned know the statutes and, every day, see the evidence on their land that observing them is only to their own good.

3. Killing is His Business (1969)

"I like to fight. I am a fighter. Once you've tasted blood, you want more blood. . . .

"Eventually there won't be enough wars. I can't kid myself . . . one day it will have to stop. That's why I'm going back to Africa. Once, in the Congo, I had a great quantity of diamonds which was taken off me. I know where there are more. I want to get those diamonds. I want to sell them and then, I think, I won't have to worry about my memories. . . .

"I want my money . . . but I fear death, I'm scared of dying. It would be a shame to have a quarter or half a million dollars' worth of diamonds in my hands and to know I've got the stuff now and yet still to go into action and to die, to get shot in Biafra, to die in that filthy, stinking, lousy place with all my riches. . . .

"I've fought for something, I've won, and I'm proud of what I am. If I am called on the mat, I will say truthfully, 'What I am, I am.' You can't take that away. There's no reason to lie or to beat around the bush. What I am, I am."

A mercenary. John Stuart Mitchell, born and raised in Montreal, is a man whose gun and guts are for hire at a high price. Twice he was out on six-month "contracts" in the Congo, and now he's fulfilling one fighting for Colonel Ojukwu in Biafra. He will fight a lot, kill a lot and in six months come out of Biafra—*if* he comes out—with about $18,000 deposited in bank accounts in South Africa and Switzerland. Also, there is loot. If you go out on a "push" to liberate a town, one building on the map of the town will be marked with a large "B" for bank and another with a "P" for post office. The bank and the post office will also have to be liberated. Or, as everywhere in Africa, there will be merchants from India who in times of distress always translate their money into diamonds and gold. The merchants will be relieved of their burden.

John Mitchell went to Rosemount High in Montreal and remembers it as a pleasant place where he had lots of friends and excelled in physical education and the sciences. He liked reading books on science. His other reading consisted of adventure magazines. After graduation he got a job, at $200 a month, learning to operate IBM machines. He worked hard and seemed on the way to carving out a comfortable career for himself, when he got the urge to travel. Once, he had seen a documentary film on South Africa and he decided that was where he wanted to go. The film dealt with the country's national parks and the wildlife that flourishes there. John always had, and has today, an immense liking for animals. At one point he even thought of becoming a mammalogist. In the talks—raw tales, many of them—we had about his experiences in the Congo, there were two incidents that visibly upset him again. He recalled angrily watching United Nations troops from India, lounging about in a square in Albertville, shoot up a dog just for sport and target practice. Another time, he and fellow mercenaries helped evacuate a group of Belgian families living on a plantation. The Belgians, clutching their most precious possessions, were loaded into a truck and about to be driven off, when John went back to have one more look around the white men's houses to make sure no one had been left behind. He saw no people, but did find several abandoned dogs wandering about. He was furious. The dogs didn't have a chance. Unable to feed themselves, never having learned to hunt, they would shortly die of starvation or be killed by the animals in the nearby jungle. If he had known the Belgians would do this to their dogs, John said, he wouldn't have risked the lives of his men in preventing their capture by the so-called Simbas, meaning lions in Swahili, led by a self-appointed general named Olinga.

He was in South Africa about a year, working now in Johannesburg at $400 a month as an IBM computer operator, when he spotted an ad in the *Rand Daily Mail* for young, healthy men not afraid of danger and willing to travel. He applied and was interviewed the next day. John spoke fluent French (he also speaks Polish, Spanish, Afrikaans and can make himself understood in five native languages) and this, he was told, was to his advantage. It was explained that the job was to go and fight in the Congo, where people speaking French were badly needed. His commanding officer would be Colonel John Peters, head of 5th Commando, a force of about 125 men made up of white South Africans and Rhodesians and now, with John and one other man, two Canadians. John believes that he and the other man, whom he prefers to be nameless, are the only Canadian mercenaries in the world. Congo President Mobutu wanted them to liberate and "clean up" the northeastern region of the Congo held by the Simbas. John, not yet 23, that same day signed up at $300 a week to join the ranks of the most feared men in Africa. He had never shot a gun in his life and didn't have a day's military experience, but because of his French he was promptly made a full lieutenant. Three and a half days later he was in an Alitalia plane on his way to Leopoldville in the Congo. From there he was flown to Stanleyville on his way to Albertville to pick up his kit. During the stopover he was taken on a sight-seeing tour of the city and came to a bridge, the Tsopolo bridge, and there, suddenly, he faced the reality of what he'd become involved in. Beneath him, everywhere he looked, the banks of the river were covered with chopped off, and now shrivelled, hands and arms, legs and feet, and the odd head. Four months before, 17 priests, 24 nuns and nearly

1,000 black men had been killed and then butchered here by the Simbas, their dismembered bodies pitched into the river. John leaned over the edge of the bridge and vomited.

In the next six months (January to July 1965) and again during his second contract (July 1966 to January 1967), John saw so much death and killing and blood and pain it becomes difficult for an ordinary man to understand. During the first contract he saw action only once, as he was mostly on liaison duty between the Congolese high command and the mercenaries. The second time—when he went up as captain of the 30-man Force Tiger—he was in the thick of the action. Personally, he shot 46 men and one child. Between 50 and 55 people were executed by his order. At this time neither side in the Congo fighting ever took prisoners. The mercenaries, for purposes of getting information, always interrogated prisoners first. They beat them with homemade "knuckle dusters" and sometimes hung them by their toes or fingers to make them talk. In John's experience, no matter how much the man was hurt, no Simba ever talked. Then the prisoners were shot. The Simbas, for their part, after first tearing the liver out of a prisoner and eating it to gain his "power," then often tortured him to death, usually by cutting him in pieces. During John's term of command, Force Tiger killed approximately 550 people: about 500 men, 40 to 50 women and four children.

John sums up the killing this way:

"In a nutshell, I had no remorse whatsoever. I knew that the Simba who gets away today, tomorrow might kill you, as an individual . . . not my men or anyone else, me, personally. So I couldn't have any remorse. It was a question of the more of them I killed the fewer had a chance to kill me."

What about the reason for being there in the first place?

"Pure and simple—money. Money only. Nothing else."

But the money came dear. Today he has memories that hurt in his head.

"I used to be musically inclined . . . but now I don't dare . . . music upsets me now because it brings back memories. If they're good memories, it's lovely, but if they're bad, it's terrible. My hands sweat. If I hear Brahms I think right away . . . a drumming sensation . . . I'm back in Africa, back shooting. . . . In those days one didn't even think of murder or killing, it just had to be done, finished, that's all. But nowadays it comes back to you slowly, you know, that you've finished off the line of a certain individual you've murdered when perhaps you didn't have to murder . . . the worst thing is that you probably killed some innocent little kid who really wasn't a spy at all, although you couldn't tell at the time. This is the penalty I'm paying now for being a mercenary. Many nights I wake up in a deep sweat, just about seeing that African's face—I *do* see his face. . . . I see a few women's faces, and that blasted little kid's face keeps bothering me every once in a while. So this is the penalty I'm paying for being a mercenary . . . when you leave the Congo or wherever with a lot of money, you have a gay time and you don't even remember these things, but when you're quiet for a little while it all comes back to you. That's why I desperately want to get to Biafra to be in action again, where you must think of the future, of today, of preservation. These things that happened in the past don't even come into your mind at all. Which is true . . . after the first few people who died, as you kill more, you don't even remember the first ones. But if you keep still and you're not in action any more, these things do come back to you. . . ."

For instance?

"The very, very first time I killed. This, I think, sticks more in my mind than any slaughter. We've been involved in a lot of slaughter, a lot of individual killings, a lot of executions. But the very first person I shot . . . well, it's hard to say what the African's age was, but I'd say he was about 30 or 32 . . . he was running at me with his spear. Not being used to an FN—I didn't have my revolver at this time—I had left it by accident on fully automatic and, of course, instead of squeezing off one shot . . . when I pulled the trigger about four or five shots went off before I released. He was peppered full of bullets from just above his navel to his Adam's apple. He died instantly. He didn't suffer. He dropped straight away . . . it was a month and a few days after my birthday, around June 24, 1965. It was the first man I had killed. The first time it's a matter of shooting him, going over to check him . . . and, of course, I felt a bit of pride, too. I was oblivious to everything. If there'd been other natives around . . . ! But that evening back in camp, in my quarters, I was by myself, coming back from a small drinking spree. I looked at the rifle standing in the corner and then it came back to me: Well, he's dead now, he's shot.

"That night I was sleepless. I kept thinking about him and this went on for three nights. He's dead now. I killed him. The sleeping pills I had taken with me I finished all off in those three days. I can envision him perfectly . . . he had a few pimples on his face. He wore a lion's cap, a tawdry thing, a piece of lion's skin hung over his forehead like a man who has his hair down like I have mine now . . . as I say, that I will never forget. I didn't commit a crime. I shot him because he was attacking me. Funny enough, the fourth day wasn't as bad, it sort of just passed my mind. But now, every once in a while, when you have a few drinks, your mind wanders to this chap . . . he probably had some kids and wives, and I've stopped his line. That's what I think about: *I've stopped his line.*"

The Simbas were unbelievably naive about fighting, John said. Sometimes they would attack the mercenaries, high and wild on *bungy,* a kind of marijuana but more potent, screaming, *"Mai! Mai!"* Always in the rear, the witch doctors urged the men on, also screaming, *"Mai! Mai!"* It means water, in Swahili, and the witch doctors had told the warriors that the white man's bullets would hit their bodies and roll off just like drops of water. And so they stormed on, screaming and shooting their guns off into the air because it wasn't the bullets but the noise the guns made that killed. And they ran into coolly aiming and firing mercenaries who mowed them down like hay. Sometimes the Simbas would send women into battle first, reckoning the mercenaries would shoot all their bullets into the women and then, when they came, there wouldn't be any left. To their dismay, there were always more bullets. It is the faces of these women John sometimes remembers at night.

And once, while out on a push, Captain Mitchell and his 30 men met a little African boy standing by the side of the road. The Simbas sometimes sent children out to size up the enemy, and then come back and report. The kid just looked at the white men, his big brown eyes wide open, trusting. He was smiling. If the boy was spying and got back to the Simbas there would be time for them to set up an ambush, or kill off white civilian prisoners, or fix trip mines further up the road. There was a decision for Captain Mitchell to make. He looked at the boy, said a few words in Swahili and pointed to something in the trees in back of the boy.

"It had to be done, but it was bad. I couldn't look him straight in the eye. As I made him turn around, I was approximately ten paces from him, and a 9-mm of course makes a big hole . . . so it was a question of raising the gun, cocking, shooting. There was very little left of the head. We used dum-dum bullets and they expand as they hit."

During John's term of command there were three other such incidents.

"After that one child I never shot any more. Of course, I could have ordered my men, 'Take him out and shoot him' . . . but it wasn't just a question of respect from the men, I wouldn't have them do what I wouldn't do myself. And it's not a question of whether I would do it again. I would. If faced with the circumstances I would *have* to do it again."

During his second contract in the Congo, there were three occasions when John was almost killed. The most severe was when his force walked into a trip mine. Three of his men were torn to pieces and died instantly, one lay screaming on the jungle path with his stomach ripped open, and John got 17 small pieces of shrapnel in the body and seven in the face.

John Mitchell is the recipient of the highest medal the Congolese government can bestow on a soldier, *La medaille de valeur extraordinaire*, of which there have been only five given out.

One day having deployed his force on tasks elsewhere, he set out, accompanied only by a sergeant, to investigate a report that Simbas were holding a group of nuns and priests prisoner in a nearby mission. At the mission the two encountered a force of 18 heavily armed Simbas.

There was a short skirmish. Then the Simba officer in charge asked to talk to John. By quick thinking, strong talk and sheer nerve John frightened the black men into surrendering the prisoners and getting out of the territory. Then he sent the nuns and priests on their way to Leopoldville. The story came to the attention of General Bobozo, number two man in the Congolese army. (One of the nuns told him that the mercenary captain should be made a saint.) The general in turn told President Mobutu. A week or so later John was ordered to report to the capital where, after a parade through town in a convertible, the president himself, in a room in his mansion filled with officers of the rank of colonel and up, pinned the medal on John and kissed him on both cheeks.

The president said that the captain had risked his life beyond and above the call of duty, that he must love the Congo, that he was glad to have people like him helping the Congo, and that there should be more like him.

The president, in uniform, then stepped back and saluted John. John returned the salute, thanked the president, said that he was very happy, that he would do it again, and that the president could call on him any time he needed him.

John Mitchell was in Canada recently for a few days to visit his parents. Now he is in Biafra, fighting. He is a man—somehow, not a *young* man—in a hurry. He wants to get rich quick. When he came out of the Congo the last time in January, 1967, he had about $30,000 in cash. He lives well and buys only the best but he is cautious and has invested in various small businesses in Africa. He is determined to retire somewhere in southern Africa when he comes out of Biafra.

John is not a simple man; he is not very much like the man next door. You wouldn't quickly say, "He's one of us." In conversation, it seemed sometimes as if he was talking about someone else. The warm, strong voice and the infectious laugh, often directed at himself, lent a kind of unreality to his stories of man's brutality to man.

A stranger walking in might say here's a man with an excellent memory, a rich vocabulary, who seems sensitive and sensible, humorous, gentle-mannered, observant, candid, alert, curious, and is unusually intelligent. And the stranger would be right. But if he asked John Mitchell:

"What are you?"

The answer would be:

"A mercenary."

4. The Friendliest Giant (1969)

Once upon a time, not long ago and from not far away, the Friendly Giant came to our land. First seen in May, 1958, he's been with us ever since. You can catch him, and his friends Rusty, a rooster, and Jerome, a giraffe, on the CBC national television network, every weekday at 10:30 a.m. CBC says it is the longest continuous show for "preschoolers" in North America, which probably means for the rest of the world as well.

Bob Homme (pronounced Hommie), 49, born and raised in Stoughton, Wisconsin, weighing 190 pounds, six feet tall, is the Friendly Giant. He owns the 15-minute show, writes it, acts and plays music in it. He works from a tiny apartment he uses as an office across from CBC's Toronto studios on Jarvis Street. It's a comfortably cluttered place: lived-in chairs and chesterfield, filing cabinets, a littered desk, a bookcase with 527 children's books, and an electric typewriter from which the letter "z" has been missing for four years.

"After I got out of the army I went to the University of Wisconsin, graduated in economics, then joined the university's radio station. That's where the Friendly show was born. Esther, my wife, and I thought it up together. The first showing, on the educational television network, was on May 4, 1953—and we haven't changed the format in 16 years.

"First came the idea of a giant, then that he be friendly, and finally that he should be *reasonable*. That's important, the reasonableness. Rusty, Jerome and I *reason* out things. Keeping the attention of the very young by giving them lots of violence and flashy action is the easy way out. Just talk to them on things they're interested in, or may be interested in, and talk straight—they'll stay with you. We take a single subject a show, talk about it, then Rusty might discover he's got a book on it, or Jerome may remember some good music or songs on it. . . .

"If the show has any special aim, it's to convey the idea that knowing about music, the outdoors, foreign countries, animals, painting, books, is a good way to be; that it's fun. To learn to enjoy acquiring new words, new sounds . . . the enjoyment of music!" The show has won Homme a number of awards: among others, four times the coveted University of Ohio award for educational television, children's category, and the Sylvania award given out by TV columnists in the U.S. It's not difficult to get addicted to the program. Friendly's mail shows that children do, but so do their mothers, some fathers, bachelors and spinsters, and a lot of grandmothers.

Bob and Esther live in a comfortable house in a new Toronto suburb with their children Richard (Dick), 19, Ann, 16, Ruth, 13, Peter, 10, and Tod, the dog, and Cat, the cat. There's also "our place in the country," a shack on 50 acres of land the farmer-owner never could find a use for, off a lonely gravel road, 77 miles east of Toronto.

On a Saturday afternoon, with the stove on, hamburgers, pickles, tea and Scotch on the table, snow piled high outside, it's a quiet, good place to be.

"You know," says Bob, "I do what I do because that's all I can do. I like it, though, and I've been lucky enough to find people who like what I do.

"It's possible that if I tried to exploit the show in a big way, syndicate it all over the place, I'd make a lot more money. But I think I'd have to change me too, then . . . I don't particularly want to change. I'd also have to work a lot more, and there's all that fishing and golfing to take care of!"

Esther is there, but she doesn't say much, it's all about Bob after all. But she listens, and it's obvious that she really likes her husband's sense of humor. Pity it's the quiet kind, understated, that never comes off if you try to quote it.

"Rusty, the rooster," explains Bob, "is sincere, a bit naive and gets his knowledge mostly from books. Jerome, the giraffe, is loud, ebullient, you like him but you see through him. He gets his information roaming the world. Now and then he has to be hospitalized—he's had half-a-dozen new ears and at least a couple of dozen new necks.

"Rod Coneybeare has handled them for the last 10 years. He's very good. Our scripts are usually just one-page outlines I write on what we're going to talk about. I lead off. Once with Rusty and Jerome in the castle we wing it. This takes a special kind of understanding, between Rod and me, and instinctively being able to follow each other's thought trends. Luckily we have it.

"Anyway, you'll see how we work on Monday. . . ."

Monday, 8:15 a.m., Studio 2, CBC-TV, Jarvis Street. This is where Stanley Burke reads the 11 o'clock news. But now Friendly is the star. They're going to tape his 2,026th show.

The big hall is crammed with lights and cameras and cables and people and Friendly Giant sets. Today the script calls for a harbour scene with lighthouse, fishing boats at anchor, warehouses, homes, all miniature. The castle stands by itself in a corner: pink, two-and-a-half-feet high with seven turrets topped with seven little yellow flags. Off to the right on the floor of the main set, the window where Friendly, Jerome and Rusty always gather, is the living room with its tiny hearth, table and three chairs.

They're pre-recording the music for today's show. Cheerful Newfoundland music. Friendly, already in costume (leather boots, brown tights, red shirt, golden tunic, wide suede belt with huge buckle, hair in a rough bang across forehead) with his recorder, Mary Syme, who has made the arrangements, at the piano, and Howie Reay on the drums. The cats Angie and Fiddle, handled by puppeteers Gustav Harsfai and Nina Keogh, will play the piano and drums on the show.

Sam Perepelkin, the floor director, is calling for quiet. Script assistant Bettina Bradley stands in a corner by herself, stopwatch in hand. Upstairs in the control booth, producer Hedley Reed begins his workday. He's been doing Friendly for two years and loves it.

The musicians start in on "I'se The B'y," then "Jack Is Every Inch a Sailor," finally "Soldier, Soldier." They're just rehearsing and camera men and other crew hum along, some go into a hop and a skip. In her corner, Bettina is dancing straight out.

By 10 the music is on tape, they're through the first rehearsal and now it's "script conference" time in the make-up room.

The girl doing Friendly's face says the bags under his eyes are getting worse. He says, "I didn't sleep well last year." You notice his whole face folds when he smiles, mouth out, cheeks up and away, narrowing the blue eyes. Rod Coneybeare is there sitting in a barber chair, and so is Hedley Reed. Rod smokes a cigar, Hedley a cigarette. Friendly gave up smoking two week ago, and feels miserable. For a while they discuss the proper pronunciation of Newfoundland—then it's time to go back. Rod says: "It'll be hard to capture the *gruelling* nature of one of our script conferences in print."

Back in the studio, John Duncan, who has played the harp on the show since it came to Canada, remarks on Rod Coneybeare's skill with the puppets, especially the incredible coordination he's able to give Jerome. Rod stands behind the castle wall, explains John, has a microphone attached to his throat and watches what he's doing on a monitor. Once a floor director got so caught up in Jerome's antics, he directed his time signals at the puppet's head. And there was a boom man who lowered his mike to Jerome and Rusty to get better sound from *their* mouths.

After dress rehearsal, the final taping. Camera on Friendly towering over harbour. He talks about the Atlantic provinces, something about gulls, and boat engines, the fishermen coming home, he guesses. Then . . .

And we're on our way to the castle. I'll hurry over first and go in the back door so I can let the drawbridge down and open the big front doors for you. Are you ready? Here's my castle.

Always the same words. Slow shot moving in on castle. The pace of the Friendly show must be the most leisurely on television. The drawbridge comes down slowly. You hear the faintest creak. Doors open to castle interior, the living room. Huge hand moves tiny pieces of furniture. . . .

Here we are inside, and here's a little chair for one of you, and a bigger chair for two more to curl up in, and for someone who likes to rock, a rocking chair in the middle.

Always the same.

Now look up . . . look waaaaay up.

Close-up of Friendly, smiling. He is truly enormous.

I'll call Rusty.

Rusty and Friendly exchange greetings. Jerome is whistled for. More greetings. Every day again, they're glad to see each other. They decide to have a concert, a Newfoundland concert, because Jerome visited there this morning. Angie and Fiddle take up their places. Rusty hands Friendly his recorder. Jerome, who always conducts, gives the signal:

Watch my nose!

Off they go full strength into "I'se The B'y."

The man under the hard lights, his grey hair mussed, looks up at the giraffe ecstatically bobbing and swinging back and forth to the music; the giraffe nudges its head against him for a moment, then whacks it back up again. The man points his recorder up at the rooster hanging in a sack from the wall, he nods at the cats banging away on the miniature piano and drum. His eyes narrow from the smile that is folding his cheeks. No one on the floor of the studio stirs. All eyes are on that tiny, intimate, warm scene. So gentle and so friendly. This giant and his friends in their castle making music, making merry, just enjoying themselves, just thoroughly enjoying themselves. And so are you.

Too soon, the cow has to make its jump over the moon behind the castle, as Friendly and John Duncan play the show's soft, slightly sad theme, the old English folksong, "Early One Morning."

There'll be a short break, and then everybody will get ready to do show No. 2,027.

Bob Homme, don't you ever get bored with Friendly?

"No. Never."

5. The Death of Don Messer's Jubilee (1969)

. . . A necessary change is the cancellation of the Don Messer series and its replacement in the opening sked for the fall and winter by the Singalong Jubilee series. The reasoning for this is to inject a fresh new element into the wintertime sked and provide a program with a younger look and younger orientation. While we recognize the values of Don Messer in the past we feel quite definitely that this change will be in the interest of the overall sked.

--Doug Nixon, Director of CBC Entertainment Programming

So they axed *Don Messer's Jubilee.* Ten years on CBC's national television network, three in the Maritimes, and before that more than 20 on CBC radio—and just like that, it's all over. The last show went on June 20, although a private station has plans to syndicate the program.

The telegram, sent from Toronto to Halifax, was dated April 14. Eventually it landed on the desk of Bill Langstroth, producer of the Don Messer show, and he had the unhappy, awkward chore of telling Don (awkward because Bill also happens to be the star and host of *Singalong*).

Don Messer talks quietly in the wall-to-wall carpeted silence in the living room of his small home on the outskirts of Halifax. He is a slim, neat, serious man, with thinning grey hair. "The news took a long, long time to sink in," he says slowly.

"I would've liked to retire with dignity and honour after 35 years—but they didn't leave me that. Strange. . . .

That's the strongest word he has for what's happened—strange. He was "used rather strangely." As he sees it he was "dropped without concrete excuse or reason." What's broadcasting all about, he wants to know, but pleasing the people? And what else has the group been doing all these years? The people, he says, liked it. In the first two weeks after the announcement he got more than 1,000 letters at home (the total number of letters received by CBC protesting cancellation at the time of writing is 7,500, including about 500 petitions).

"When we're gone, our kind of music just won't be around anymore. *Singalong* doesn't have it, *Tommy Hunter* doesn't, and neither does *Pig and Whistle.*"

Gone means two days ahead, Thursday evening, May 8, when, as things stand now, they will tape the last, the very last, *Don Messer's Jubilee.*

* * * * *

Thursday evening, and they are all there for dress rehearsal in Studio 1 on Bell Road. Beneath a ceiling of 160-odd lamps, wandering among the cables and cameras and microphones, you see some of the most familiar faces in the country. Don himself, looking neat and debonair in a light grey suit, red tie, red handkerchief in his breast pocket. The boys in the orchestra wear the same thing. There's Duke Nielsen, bass, who's been with Don 37 years; Waldo Munro, piano; Vic Mullen, banjo; Rae Simmons, sax and clarinet; Warren MacRae, drums; and Cec McEachren, guitar and violin. They're having a birthday party for Don at Cec's home after the show. Don will be 60 tomorrow. In a porch swing, studying his lines, is Don Tremaine, the announcer. Johnny Forest, the Scottish singer, wearing his kilt, is talking with some kids on a tour of the building. One of tonight's guests, singer George Longard, is tuning his big red guitar. Marg Osburne is chatting with the other guest, step-dance champion Wendy Morris, age 10. Marg smiles as you come up to her. Marg smiles a lot. She is one of the smilingest, warmest, sincerest ladies you'd ever want to meet.

"I just wouldn't think of retiring and going home now," she says. "It would be such an alone and empty feeling. I like entertaining. When I'm in front of that camera I'm singing to all those people out there."

And then:

"Did you know that in Teasdale, Ontario, a lot of people are driving around with car stickers saying Teasdale Wants Messer? Isn't that nice?"

But where's old Charlie? Charlie Chamberlain. When you talked to him the first time you thought of Zorba the Greek. Zorba, too, was very much his own man. Charlie is sitting out on the stairway, having a smoke, thinking, looking miserable. He says he has to fly to Winnipeg right after the show for some "public relations". That means he'll miss the party at Cec's as well as the one CBC is throwing later. He also says he's moving back to Belledune, New Brunswick. But Charlie doesn't really feel like talking so, being Charlie, he just shuts up.

In the control booth, Cy True is producing. By now most of Bill Langstroth's time is taken up with *Singalong Jubilee*. Cy says afternoon rehearsals went pretty well, but the cast was just a bit off, not quite their usual snappy selves. They seemed preoccupied.

Maybe just angry and hurt. On the evening news there was an item to the effect that CBC president George Davidson has told the Commons broadcasting committee in Ottawa that the Don Messer show fell victim to old age. . . .

You go out and investigate. One of the Gunter Buchta dancers prepares a list of all their ages, and you gather up those of the rest of the cast. Then you add, you divide, and you come to the conclusion that the average age on the average Don Messer show is—29.

In the studio, Johnny Forest is dancing "Here We Go Round the Mulberry Bush" with the kids. Marg joins in and, lo and behold, so does the boss, Don. The dancing stops and they sing "This Land Is Your Land." Then the kids have to go because dress rehearsal is starting.

Don Tremaine on mike:

"We come to the program tonight with mixed feelings. We're sad about this being our last show on CBC television. To paraphrase Winston Churchill, 'Never have so few'"—it's very quiet now in Studio 1—"'owed so much to so many.' We are delighted that some of you have been with us for as many as 13 seasons and most happy you could join us tonight for—*Don Messer's Jubilee!*"

The Islanders swing right into eight bars of "Fireman's Reel"; Marg, Charlie and Johnny follow with "Goin' to the Barndance"; back to "Fireman's Reel," 24 bars, close-up of Don smiling down the length of his violin; and back to Don Tremaine who introduces guests George and Wendy . . . .

"And where," asks Wendy's father watching his daughter from the corner where we visitors huddle, "is young talent now going to get a chance around here?"

Charlie lumbers up to centre stage for his solo still looking miserable. He takes a deep breath, smiles a little, and gives off with "Any Time You're Feeling Lonely."

Lester Sellick is in our corner, a retired naval officer who is writing a biography of Don Messer. He says he is doing it because Don is "a Canadian who has made a great cultural contribution to his country." He is here to record "this historic moment" with his Polaroid camera.

After each number there's a break of a couple of minutes and it's then that you notice how close this group is; tonight perhaps more so. They howl and hoot and tease. They smile a lot at each other. This is home. They are in their living room. They like Charlie's singing, and Marg's and Johnny's, and they like the guests and the Buchta dancers. It doesn't matter that they've been going like this for 10 years. They know that out there in the big land people enjoy them carrying on this way. And they are pros. There'll be no sour faces, no angry speeches, a few jokes maybe about going out and selling pencils tomorrow and 'What time is rehearsal next week, Don?' But that's all. There's a job to do. A show to tape. It will be another smooth, fast-paced *Don Messer's Jubilee*.

Marg is well into "Vaya Con Dios" when you're introduced to a man sitting in a wheelchair. He is Bill Campbell, 37, who was a cameraman on the show until he contracted multiple sclerosis in 1963 and had to leave CBC. He comes to every Messer rehearsal and taping.

"I'm going to miss it so damn much," he says.

The orchestra and dancers are on with a number called "Whistling Rufus." Bill watches them and says:

"You know, when I hear that music I'd like to do a little song and dance myself." He smiles reassuringly.

"All up in my head, of course."

He looks back at the dancers slapping and bowing and whirling.

Johnny follows with an old rouser called "Keep Right On to the End of the Road"; a very composed Wendy Morris step-dances her way through "Spring Carnival Hornpipe"; George Longard sits on a white bench under a tree and sings to "Molly Darlin'"; the dancers do the Zaparosica. The orchestra comes up behind with "Grandma's Chickens"; then Marg sings "May the Good Lord Bless and Keep You" and means every word of it. Don Tremaine steps up to the mike, thanks the guests, and ends with: "Thank you for being with us these past all-too-brief years."

Between rehearsal and final taping there's a short meeting in the conference room upstairs. There isn't much to discuss tonight, the show is tight and neat. Cy True says he would like to thank all of them for their help and co-operation and would they please all try to stay for the party afterwards. Then he says: "And now let's go down and show 'em how it's done!"

Everybody applauds and Don Messer says quietly, "Hear! Hear!"

During final taping it's best to stay out of the way. You find a chair next to make-up girl Caroline Aldred who is back her first day after being off with a broken arm. As you watch, and watch others watching, it comes again, this feeling of home, of fun, of a big family of unpretentious people having a whale of a good time. Home is what the show is all about. Home is Messer's bag.

Quite suddenly, it's all over. The last Don Messer show is on tape.

A CBC public relations man is herding cast and production crew together for pictures. Maybe 60 people are bunched together.

Three long tables covered with white paper are being set up in the centre of the studio. Food is unloaded from boxes—pickles, chips, crackers, bread, three kinds of cheese, four kinds of meat. There is sherry for the ladies, and two huge washtubs full of ice and cans of beer. The party is on. Cameramen and propmen and wardrobe ladies and lighting engineers come up to Don Messer and say, "Goodbye Mr. Messer, it's been good working with you all these years." And he shakes their hands and smiles. Syd Kennedy, director for the

CBC Maritimes, climbs up on the stage. He says nobody is here to say goodbye to Don Messer, only farewell. He himself, he says, doesn't agree with CBC's decision but by the same token the person who has this kind of decision to make must make it and shouldn't be second-guessed. He talks about his long association with Don Messer, 31 years. He sees him going with much, much regret. It's a good party.

But it's past 11 now and time to go to the other one. Cec has invited you and Don Messer offers a lift in his 1962 red Thunderbird. Cec's home is across the harbour in Dartmouth. The wives are all there, in Cec's basement rec room, serving biscuits with egg salad and Scotch with ginger ale. At exactly midnight Cec's wife comes down the stairs with a white and pink cake with a violin on it in brown icing and 12 candles. Everybody stands up and sings Happy Birthday Dear Donald. Duke Nielsen takes out his camera and films Don unwrapping his present. It's a new violin case lined with red velvet. A little plaque on the outside says "To Don on his 60th from The Islanders" and their first names.

This is a good party, too.

Later, driving back to Halifax, you think about the parties and how, though they did the last, the very last, *Don Messer's Jubilee* tonight, it seemed as if everybody was having a pretty good time.

And then you remember that after the final taping, they wheeled Bill Campbell out of Studio 1, weeping.

6. The Man They Love to Hate (1971)

He bounced up from behind his desk and shook hands warmly. Then Vancouver's mayor Tom Campbell lifted his right leg and pointed to three dark spots on his pants just above the knee. He had cut his finger the night before, he explained, repairing one of the old clocks he collects. It was only a tiny cut, but the Band-Aid had just come off, and some of the blood had dropped on his trousers . . . .

Thus, a fast, first impression: a friendly, down-to-earth man with a nice, quiet hobby. Probably accurate, probably not contrived. But the mayor is very, very good at creating impressions. He does it with simple words and gestures which promptly turn into headlines. He does it spontaneously, instinctively, ceaselessly, and it has just about made his name a household word in Canada. In the end, though, he leaves you a bit flat. Because what you have are just that—impressions. Some probably true, many others debatable. You're not sure whether the picture they form comes even close to showing who he really is. But if somehow it does, you're left to wonder, inevitably, if that's *all* he is. It's an interesting point.

"When will the story come out?" he asked, as we sat down in his mahogany-panelled office in city hall.

I said not until well after the election, still some weeks away.

"Fine," the mayor said, and hurled himself at the red phone behind his desk.

Campbell, who is 43, does everything fast. Thinking, talking, walking—as if striding through high grass—moving his eyes and hands. Sometimes all that speed is almost violent. He is a big, healthy-looking, handsome man with thick, graying hair that grows fairly long in back and wide sideburns. His clothes are expensive, colourful, stylish and slightly rumpled. His face glows and jumps. He exudes energy. I remember thinking he'd go berserk in 24 hours in solitary.

"It's me, dear," he said, the words rushing out. "He says not till after the ninth—OK? Right! Yes, yes, yes. Bye!"

"My wife," he explained. "She wants to be sure it won't appear before. Best political adviser in the world. Very astute. We live the job 24 hours a day. If Julie was running she'd be the only politician in town I'd be afraid of. She'd beat the *pants* off me!"

And Campbell laughed his laugh. He laughed often. It started with the upper lip curling, then tentatively pulling back in a soundless snarl. Then the mouth would break open and this full, hearty braying would explode. He could sustain the laugh quite long or cut it abruptly. But if he was actually often amused, I couldn't tell.

Once he was, though. Talking about his children, he said that the oldest had hair down to *here,* indicating his shoulders. My eyes must have lit up. This man had done more public denouncing of long-haired kids than anybody else in the country. That's what he was *famous* for—"If they won't work, *let 'em starve!"* And here *he* had a son. . . .

"Yeah, it really looks great on *her!"* he yelled, and broke up.

The phone rang and Campbell jumped for it.

"Bill! How are you? Yes! Phone his office . . . go ahead! Now I want lots of work out of you, Bill—not money, mind!—*work*. OK, OK, OK. Bye!"

In the two working days I spent with the mayor he asked me to leave his office only once, because the aldermen wanted an *in camera* meeting there. Otherwise, I sat in on all phone calls and visitors, and accompanied him on various chores around the city. When he wasn't talking to others he was talking to me. Except for one or two small matters to do with entirely private affairs, he never once said, "This is off the record," nor, for that matter, "No comment."

"From the moment I leave the house in the morning," he said, "everything I do is public—until I shut that door again at night."

He talked in short sentences of mostly little words. And he always listened as closely as I did to *how* he sounded.

"The name of the game," he started right off, "is being *known*. I can gauge my stock from how people respond on the sidewalks when I'm in a parade or something. I was even recognized once in front of Buckingham Palace!

"I'm acutely conscious of print. Yes, the press hurts at times—but you *can't* let 'em see blood. Once only in nine years I called an editor about a misquote.

"This is a tough, tough game. The image is all important. Not the politics, but the *man*. Look at Reagan, he went from actor to politician—they *go* together, acting and politics."

One of the things people called him was "Canada's Ronald Reagan." Did he mind?

"Ronald Reagan got re-elected," he said, and his lip curled.

"I like open-line shows, but they're getting a bit rigged now. I love TV. I'm not good at making speeches, but I'm good at repartee: I think fast. I keep everything in black and white. "

But *surely* there was . . .?

"Black and white is much easier to understand," he said.

Then followed some information: Campbell is a lawyer. He is a self-made multimillionaire from real-estate development in Vancouver—"I built half this town." The Campbells like to vacation in Hawaii; they've been there 14 times. They are not joiners. They don't go to nightclubs. Every Saturday night they have a meal out. Every Sunday his in-laws come over for a family dinner. His father was a policeman in Vancouver. He doesn't hunt or fish because he doesn't like to kill things. He once tried secretly to learn dancing from Arthur Murray but failed dismally because of poor coordination; same thing with water skiing. He stays fit by "fast talk and fast footwork." He never carries keys, money or identification. His salary as mayor is $20,000. He was a two-pack-a-day smoker but quit "four years, four months, one day, three hours and 20 minutes ago." He expected the campaign to cost $30,000 and added, "This is definitely my last term." He has a girl and two boys, aged eleven, eight and seven. Some time back the newspapers started calling him Tom Terrific—"I love that name now." He had never before permitted taking pictures in his home—we would be the first. His regular reading is the local papers and *Popular Mechanics*—"The nation could be bankrupt for a month and I wouldn't know."

"You know," said the mayor, "I feel a terrible responsibility to do a good job here. Isn't that what life is all about? Accomplishing things? Doing things? I like the good things, but I don't believe in living in the lap of luxury. . . . We have no help in the house, you know. Julie does it all on her own."

And from there, naturally, to hippies.

"What makes me so mad," he said, "is that they won't help themselves. I feel sorry for them. They complain they haven't got employment—but look at them! Who would hire them? They are a lost generation.

"They are a lost generation," he repeated, rolling the words, listening to them.

"We've got to get them before they get lost. . . . They're always talking about 'doing their own thing.' Well, I went down to one of our beaches and I went up to them and I said, 'What is your own thing?' And they couldn't answer me!

"Next summer they're going to be like locusts across the country," he said.

Yes, and an awful lot of kids probably would be heading for Vancouver again. What was he going to do?

"I don't know, I don't know," he said. "It's a phase they're going through—I hope." Then he brightened. "But I believe, just the same, that our young people are a step to tomorrow. . . . You've got to use that! Our young people are a step to tomorrow."

I came back to hippies several times but, in essence, that's what he had to say about them.

The phone rang often; visitors dropped in; we drove here and there in his limousine; we ate together twice; he sparred with the local press; he showed me around his beautiful, $100,000 home. Through it all he was friendly, down-to-earth and giving impressions.

Four big men in their late 50s with deep voices and small mustaches sat across the mayor's desk. They wore suits with vests and expensive shoes. Top executives from one of the most powerful business associations in Canada, they'd come to pay their respects.

"You're on the eve of an election, then," one of them opened.

"Maybe on the eve of disaster," said the mayor and laughed his laugh.

Some more pleasantries and then:

"How's the labour situation, Mr. Mayor?"

"Much better," said the mayor.

The talk drifted to unemployment, to the Maritimes where they refuse to get industrialized, where people just want to fish and hunt and not worry.

"They don't give a damn," said one of the executives.

"It's called 'doing your thing,'" said another.

"Doing your thing," echoed a third.

The bell had rung again.

"Well, let me tell you, I went after the hippies here about 'doing their thing,'" said the mayor. "I went down to one of our beaches, and I got hold of them and I said, 'OK, now what is your thing?' And nobody could tell me what their 'thing' was. I figured out what it was; it was—not to work!"

"Right," said an executive.

"Right," echoed another.

"Sure, we can have shorter work weeks and higher pay," said the mayor. "But, you still got to produce."

"Got to produce," said an executive.

"You still got to produce," said the mayor.

"That's the key," said an executive.

"We've got a very, very high-paying province here," the mayor told his visitors. "Of course we've got everything going for us—fish, lumber, the harbour, skilled people, not too big a population, the weather. Vancouver'll go nowhere but up! We've got the whole Pacific rim opening up to us. . . . We'll become the New York of the Pacific!

"Why, even the hippie," he added, "is smart enough to know it's better in Vancouver than in a doorway in Montreal!"

"On our trip across Canada," said an executive, "we saw just thousands of them on the roads. . . ."

"Right. Right," said the mayor.

Mayor Campbell prefers to sit up front in his limousine with police driver John MacRitchie.

They were crossing one of Vancouver's bridges and passing a transport truck. For a few seconds the two vehicles ran nose to nose. The mayor turned and looked up at the driver in his cabin. He was trying to catch the driver's eye, but the man stared ahead at the road. The mayor kept looking and then the man glanced down. They were looking into each other's faces. The mayor nodded and smiled and nodded again, but the truck driver's face stayed blank and then he turned his eyes back to the road—and the limousine shot past.

It was Poppy Day and the mayor had been asked to a home for the aged to pin poppies on some of the folks and get the drive going. Forty-one men and women were sitting waiting in a circle in the lounge. They wore dark suits and pressed blouses.

They applauded when the mayor came in. At great speed he went around to all and pinned poppies, smiled, shook hands and kissed one little old fat lady on the cheek. There was only one newspaperman there. No cameras.

The mayor's little speech ended. . . .

"We're all trying to build a wonderful city here. I think we've done pretty well. And I think most of the credit has to go to our senior citizens. Today I commend you and wish you the very, very best on your poppy sale. Thank you."

As he hurried out of the home a car pulled up and a TV cameraman got out. The mayor turned and strode right back inside. Amid much laughter everybody was asked to take off their poppies. The mayor asked to have the lady he had kissed pointed out to him.

"We'll go around again," the mayor said quietly to the cameraman. "I'll stop there in front of that lady—maybe that's where you ought to stand —and we'll do the kissing again."

To the home's director he said: "Same drill. We'll just take the poppy tray . . . we'll kiss the lady . . . and that they've got to print!"

"Well, don't they!" he asked the cameraman.

And to no one in particular, he said: "And when they see it on the screen, they'll say it's phoney."

To the circle: "We'll start with that gentleman there, and go along four or five to him, there—OK?"

"Take one!" the mayor called. "Let's go!"

It became very quiet. A few of the old people giggled.

"Golly, he's marvellous with them," whispered an elderly clergyman, standing watching out of camera range.

Slowly now, the mayor moved from citizen to citizen, smiling, saying softly "How'dydo, how'dydo", and when he got to the little old fat lady he leaned over and in a dignified way gave her a small kiss on the cheek. The camera was about two feet away.

They'd have to print it.

Six reporters, "the boys," he called them, slouched into Campbell's office looking tired and grumpy. Not a fair match, somehow, for the ever-exuberant mayor. The impression was that he thought about five times as fast as they did. There was some quibbling about what he had said about the War Measures Act—old news already. He had said he wanted to use it for the pursuit of all kinds of criminals.

"I stand by it," the mayor said. "If we have a revolt here, you boys will be the first to blame me. . . . I haven't heard a word about it from Ottawa. . . . I've got good relations with Ottawa. I can phone Trudeau any time!" And he made a dramatic lunge for the phone.

"What I'm saying should have been said in Montreal seven years ago." And then, out of nowhere. "It's my responsibility to wake up the silent majority."

"You're running on Spiro's platform, Tom," said a reporter.

"It's you guys who're making me," the mayor shot back.

The mayor, always ahead, and three companions, were moving along a crowded, downtown sidewalk to get lunch. It was a five-minute walk.

"You'll see now," the mayor had said, "how they recognize me."

They strode along. One minute, two minutes, three, four, and then, just as they got to the restaurant a woman approaching with a shopping bag in each hand, smiled and said, "Hi, Tom!"

The mayor nodded and smiled and said "Howdy-do."

"See!" he said as they went in to eat.

* * * * *

The most important room in the Campbell home is quite small. There's a colour TV set with three comfortable chairs for the kids, a big chair where Julie reads and in back the mayor's workshop where he fixes his clocks. He showed some of the tiny, delicate tools he works with.

"The one most important thing in my life," he said, "is my family. I'm a family man. I don't cheat on my wife and I'm trying to raise my kids to be good kids. Isn't that what life's all about? Discipline? Democracy?"

"Material things, I suppose, are number two. Car, money, house, clothes, travel."

A bit later he went upstairs and lay down on the huge bed in the master bedroom to take a call from CBC's *Radio Free Friday*.

"Seven years ago they said in Montreal this could never, never happen," he told them in Toronto, lying flat on his back and waving a pencil. "All I'm doing is, I'm sounding the alarm in B.C., in Vancouver, that it could well happen here . . . I'm protecting the majority, not the minority."

Julie, tall and handsome, blonde and alert, watched him from the door.

"Isn't he wonderful," she whispered. "He's so sweet and gentle, you know."

It was towards the end of the second day, driving along in the limousine, the mayor up front.

He turned around and said:

"You've been in town a few days now—what are they saying about me?"

"Well, frankly, most of the people I've talked to loathe you," I said.

"Did you ask them who they were going to vote for?" the mayor wanted to know.

"Yes, I did," I said.

"Well . . .?"

"You," I said.

And the mayor smiled his smile.

During the days spent with Mayor Tom Campbell, I asked at random some 35 Vancouverites what they thought of him. Without exception, they said they didn't like him. Some replies:

A librarian: "I wish people would see through him. He's such a ham, he makes you sick."

An elevator operator: "Strange thing, a school chum of mine works with him—I don't know how he can stand it."

Wife of an advertising executive: "I know he gets headlines all the time with the silly things he says, but, you know, he's made all of us very alert and interested in what happens at city hall."

City hall reporter: "He has almost no personal friends. He uses people."

Retail store owner: "I think his law and order bit is a smoke screen for Vancouver's real problems: unemployment, pollution, housing, rapid transit, welfare, poor tax-sharing formulas with Victoria and Ottawa . . . he doesn't do much except talk."

A politician: "He's just another politician."

Taxi driver: "Some kind of nut. He doesn't know what's going on."

Restaurant operator: "This city grows no matter who runs it."

Retired surgeon: "He makes us look like fools right across the country with his wild talk."

The other thing their statements had in common was that, yeah, they'd probably vote for him. Perhaps because, as a newspaper editor put it, "He's the only game in town."

(On December 9, 1970, for the third consecutive time, Tom Campbell was elected mayor of Canada's third-largest city.)

7. Path to Yesterday (1971)

"Why do you want people to see this place?" I asked John Hillen. He is a designer of museum interiors and was holding open the door of the one he had just finished. Ste. Marie Among the Hurons, in Midland, Ontario, 95 miles north of Toronto, is the largest single-theme historical museum in North America. It took four years to build.

"Because it's beautiful," said Hillen, and we went inside.

We stepped into semi-darkness onto cobblestones—and into another world. We walked along a narrow street, faintly heard the sound of church bells, children playing, sea gulls, a horse trotting by. And a voice murmured, ". . . a town on the coast of Normandy, France. Beyond those houses lies the harbour from which Jesuit missionaries embark on their long journey to the country of the Hurons. . . ." Three hundred years had dropped away. We were *there.*

Guide Hillen said little. His textures, shapes, shadows, colours, sounds, objects and smells did the talking. A chain of environments that gradually deepened a sense of impending doom. I discovered, as we moved along, that impressions and sensations were often mere suggestions or hints. The imagination was thus set loose and I felt that much of whatever insight I got into that other time, I had acquired on my own. It was painless learning, exciting, magical even, and the world's best antidote against museum feet.

Ste. Marie's story is this: A cold and isolated spot on the shores of Georgian Bay, it was the furthest point white men had penetrated in Canada. Construction of a settlement was started in 1639 when Jesuit missionaries made it their headquarters among the Huron Wendat Nation. Ten years later the Frenchmen deliberately burned it down so it wouldn't fall into the hands of advancing Iroquois. But still seven Jesuits and thousands of Hurons were killed by the Iroquois. And with them dreams of riches, power and peace. What happened there touches the very beginnings of our background, culture and identity.

For three centuries the site lay virtually untouched. The first serious archeological investigations were begun by the Royal Ontario Museum and completed in 1951 by the University of Western Ontario. A palisaded community of more than 20 structures was revealed. Ontario's government leased the area from the Jesuit Order and, by 1967, the site had been rebuilt.

To ease a visitor to Ste. Marie from the 20th into the 17th century, he's taken through a kind of time tunnel. First a movie, showing the Jesuits living among the Hurons, building their settlement and then destroying it; next, the site itself; finally, the museum.

Hillen's assignment was to link Ste. Marie to the mainstream of history. To tell a single, flowing story that slowly builds to its tragic end. This was done by creating a multi-dimensional portrait of the French, New France, the Jesuits and the Natives and their eventual downfall. The last part of the 10,000-square-foot display area deals with the arts of archeology and history, and how the site was rebuilt.

Early on in the tour we met Hillen's colleague, artist Frances Brittain, and the three of us wandered on together. I can't describe that whole journey, but here are parts of it:

Nailed low to a wall, a 350-year-old ship's pulley worn smooth with age. It's for kids to hit and feel it turn.

A looming, split cross, dramatically symbolizing the wars of religion in Europe and what followed.

There were 22 slide and stereo tape programs, made by a young man named Marten Lewis, playing continuously throughout the museum. One of the visual shows was in a small, round theatre and depicted on three screens simultaneously the 800-mile canoe trip the Jesuits had to make from Quebec to Ste. Marie. The tape shows featured 20 different voices and were tuned so finely it *was* no strain to hear and no strain not to hear either.

Hillen: "We thought a lot about kids and their open minds when we were making this."

A quiet corner where silhouettes of Jesuits walk to and fro, reading or praying. Black robes in the wilderness.

The museum was built by the University of Western Ontario, under direction of the chairman of the Ste. Marie museum project, Vernon Mould, with Ontario government money (about $500,000) and on opening day, May 15, will be given back to the province.

A map made of stained copper shows early trade routes in diamonds, emeralds and rubies. Europe was after spices and you can smell them—pepper, ginger, cinnamon, cloves, cardamom and nutmeg.

One big reason why this country came into being is expressed in a 17th-century pamphlet: "Of all the ornaments which luxury has invented, there are none so glorious, so august and so precious as furs."

There are many walls. Walls of leather, beaver fur, cork, old barn-boards, felt, debarked mill slabs, shingles, cloth, braided corn husk malting, two-by-fours, adzed boards, bricks, little trees and big trees.

Frances Brittain: "We tried to make it so you feel it with your body, your mind and in your guts."

I see and often touch the tools, clothes, ships, coins, weapons, drawings, musical instruments, pipes, food, books, masks, paintings, buildings, pottery, furniture, jewelry and maps from that other time.

And I hear its music and words.

Roughly 100 hours had been spent discussing and planning just that entrance with the cobblestone floor.

There's a pile of seven rocks to mark the Jesuits who died. Behind are dark, bare, broken trees with a narrow beam of light piercing through from above.

The voice of an old Indian tells how it was in Wendake, Huronia. He ends: "All this truly happened long ago . . . the Hurons are no more. All that is left is the sad wind that moans about the empty fields in winter."

When we got to the end, praise was due and duly spoken. The two listened. Those kind of words were familiar. This was the third museum interior they had built together.

Hillen: "A nice thing about this job is that what you're making will stand a long time. So *many* will come through. . . ." Suddenly Hillen reached out and poked me in the chest. His gray, very innocent eyes were positively shining. "You think this is something?" he almost yelled. "Wait till the next one I do!"

And there was just no way I could argue that. Also, he's my father.

8. The Hottest Hot-liner of Them All (1971)

Ten minutes to go and then Vancouver would be quieter. Only one of the sounds of the city would be stilled—but listen:

"WEBSTAHR-R-R-R-R-R!"

That would stop. At 7:15 that Friday evening it would go away and not return until Monday at 9 a.m. Then it would sound again in the city's homes, cars, hospitals, offices, jails and parks, and pound into the ears of the people—"WEBSTAHR-R-R-R-R-R!" A roar in Scottish burr telling the world to give a damn.

Jack Webster—surely *emperor* of the radio hot-liners—leaned into his microphone and cut off a caller:

"Make your POINT, old boy!"

And somewhere, clutching a phone, "old boy" did. He spoke perhaps more concisely than ever before in his life. Wiggling about in his chair, Webster listened with forehead creasing, fingers snapping and eyes darting. He lit what may have been the day's 100th cigarette. Then he started furiously scribbling in shorthand; he underlined it, circled it, and boxed it. He listened for 30 solid seconds—and lunged at the mike again.

"THANKS, old boy!"

And "old boy" was holding a dead phone. But he'd had his say. Talked to Jack himself—and *told* him. Put in his two-bits on *City Mike*, a 45-minute call-in show that starts at 6:30 p.m. and is the little brother to *Talk Back to Webster*, which runs from 9 to 12 in the morning and is also heard Monday through Friday.

A stocky, aggressive Scot who came to Canada in 1947, Webster hosts both under contract to station CKNW of New Westminster. He operates from a cramped little studio on the mezzanine floor of the Hotel Georgia in downtown Vancouver. It's ear-shattering, controversial, fighting stuff that makes him the most listened-to man on the coast. The rest of us get him served with fair regularity on CBC-TV's *Front Page Challenge* and *Weekend.* At $100,000 a year, he is the highest-paid reporter in Canadian broadcasting.

And reporter he is—"Just a bloody REPORTER-R-R-R!" Over the years he's broken some of the biggest stories in the West, and nationally, too, and has a 17-pound book of clippings to prove it. One that comes to mind was when the House of Commons erupted last October following an interview in which Jean Marchand, minister of regional economic expansion, implied the War Measures Act had been invoked to prevent FLQ intervention in Montreal's civic elections.

Webster's hurt-looking eyes flew to the big clock on the wall—eight minutes to go—and to the three burly men across the table. Webster's eyes always look hurt—anguished sometimes. The three were union executives. A transportation strike threatened the coast. It was big news and Webster had been on it most of the day. (About 90 percent of the time he's concerned with news and public affairs, the rest is showbiz.) It was a complex issue. Shaking a finger he barked a question at the union men related to what "old boy" had just said. It was a short question, simple, to the point, shaved of all politeness. One of them answered, searching for words that sounded good. Webster interrupted and the needle on the volume metre jumped.

"IS it? Or is it NOT?"

At its best, Webster's voice is a blend of an angry Charles Laughton and an angry James Robertson Justice. At its worst it's something else: Once on a TV panel show he was able to shout down, by himself, Dalton Camp, Marcel Faribault, Eric Kierans, Paul Hellyer, David Lewis and Laurier LaPierre.

I had sat in on Webster sessions for the better part of a week and had grown accustomed to him; that is, I'd developed a fine defence mechanism. With him, I, too, talked loud and asked hard, short questions. If he took longer than 30 seconds I cut him off. Ninety seconds was about my limit for conversing on one topic. Occasionally I barked.

Another way of coping, of course, was not to listen—shut Webster off. And that's what I did those last few minutes of the show. Shut off that voice that could go like a machine gun and then suddenly gear down to a slow, malicious purr as happened one evening in the studio with Eric Kierans, the ex-minister of communications:

"As a matter of fact, Mr. Kierans, the record of the Trudeau government has not REALLY been shining regarding unemployment—has it, Mr. Kierans?"

So I shut off the voice and reviewed some of the week that was.

Webster, I had learned, starts his days at 6:05. By 8 he's downtown and having the first of 15 coffees. By 9 he's done the mail, answered a dozen calls, read the papers, taped an interview, lined up the show, and emptied the first of the five packs of cigarettes he'll smoke. And he is *jumping* to go. From 9 to 9:30 is crucial because that's when most people are listening—about 186 000. At noon he makes for a private club around the corner and plays rackets for two hours. He plays hard. I saw a match between Jack, 53, and a lean, 28-year-old banker. Jack won one out of three games. After showering he looked pleased. "Lost two pounds—all WATER-R-R-R-R-R!"

Then back to the hotel, a quick sandwich, and then phoning, talking, reading and interviewing until *City Mike* at 6.30. It's all done at breakneck speed, and his impatience is catching. The phones ring all the time. The day moves at an incredible pace; the tension never really lets up, even when Webster, on air, breaks into song or gives 'em a laugh.

Born in a Glasgow tenement, Webster quit school at 14. At 17, as a reporter on a Glasgow paper, he covered the city's gang battles. He worked for several Scottish and English newspapers until World War II, during which he served as a British army officer for five years in North Africa. When he came to Canada he got a $45-a-week job as a reporter on the *Vancouver Sun*. He rose to city editor there before going into radio in 1953.

What makes Jackie run? Well, there's money: It allows Webster and his wife Margaret (they have three adult children) to live in a big house in one of Vancouver's poshest districts. There's also a 94-acre farm bought two years ago on the side of a mountain on Salt Spring Island in the Strait of Georgia. (Incidentally, his late father once told him: "Jack, it's a piece of nonsense, what you're doing. You make more money than the prime minister of Britain!")

There's power: Webster has some of that on the coast. Even B.C.'s premier W.A.C. Bennett admits it: "Every time you criticize me, Webster, that's five more votes for us."

There's enjoyment: He obviously loves what he's doing. And it's also won him virtually every award a broadcaster can win.

And there is, in his words, "a sense of INJUSTICE": The job lets him express this and work at it to his heart's content.

It was an ordinary week and he had interviewed, in person or on the phone, 23 people, including two federal cabinet ministers and a senator. On the average he does four interviews a day. He calculated he's done 11,000 in the last 10 years. With the help of his female assistant he handled between 900 and 1,000 calls on and off the air during the five days I spent with him.

Webster's audience regards him as an unofficial ombudsman.

"People say: 'Webster'll know what to do,'" he told me. "'Webster'll tell me where to go and complain.' And they know that if I go on a campaign, I'll hammer and hammer and HAMMER—till I get ACTION!"

Modestly:

"But I only win little battles. Never big ones. Never won an election, for instance. And I've been fighting Social Credit for NINETEEN years!"

Little battles add up. Webster's 1970 "Victory List" numbers 51. They range from getting an old lady a hearing aid, finding a foster home for a child, saving trees, to being instrumental in settling a major strike.

Webster has been called a lot of names: professional loudmouth, pipsqueak, fraud, creep, louse, radiot, prostitute, stentorian vulgarian and pompous quidnunc. The week that I was in Vancouver, just in off-air time, the fink (which is what *he* likes to call people) tried to steer callers right on these matters: unemployment insurance, welfare, housing, a crooked car dealer, a missing person, legal aid, parole, desertion of a common-law husband, mental illness, a fraudulent travel agent, the Constitution, misleading advertising, workmen's compensation, abortion, alcoholism, fraud in welfare, yoga, lawyer problems, desertion of a *legal* husband, debts, drugs, loneliness, dealing with a finance company, a bottle delivery system, money stolen, police brutality, combines, drains, landlord-tenant difficulties, rent deposits, adoption, taxes, fighting city hall, septic tanks, jobs, a variety of laws, hospitalization and, "Should I leave my husband, Jack?"

Webster swiftly manipulated the push-button switchboard near him on the table. During commercials and newsbreaks he lines up callers. "Are you on the TOPIC?" he demands of each. And if they aren't, likely as not he'll go *Click!*

For instance:

Webster: "Are you on the TOPIC?"

Man's voice: "Well, Jack . . ."

Webster: "Do you want to talk to my GUEST?"

Voice: "I want to talk to you, Jack."

Webster: "Well, I don't want to talk to YOU!" *Click!*

And:

Man's voice: "Mr. Webster, I want to talk to you about my father-in-law."

Webster: "NO! Talk to me about your father-in- law tomorrow!" *Click!*

Sometimes, though, he was different:

Woman's voice: (Low, dragging the words) "I don't want to talk about what you're talking about right now."

Webster: (Gruff, but astonishingly there was a note of gentleness) "What is it, dear?"

Woman: (Sighs) "Well, it's about . . . drugs." Webster: "No, not drugs tonight. But you call me tomorrow, love—all right?" *Click!*

And again:

Old man's voice: "It's me, Pete. Remember? My wife, in January?"

Webster: "Hello, Pete."

Old man: "I was just wondering. I think I was in the army with your guest . . ."

Webster: "Yes, well Pete. I was glad to help you with the other thing, but I don't want to put you on the air with a question like that. How are you doing? All right?"

Old man: "I'm by myself . . . I'll tell you what. I'll mail you a cheque for the taxi."

Webster: "No, you won't, Pete. I have to go now."

Old man: "OK . . ."

Webster: "Right. Bye, Pete." *Click!*

"Pete was a guy who came to us for help when his wife was dying," Webster explained. "He's in a wheelchair."

That Friday night show had only about four more minutes to run, but Webster never let the momentum of questions and answers ease up. Earlier in the week, I remembered, he and I had a similar session—with *me* doing the badgering. We were coming back on the ferry from a visit to his farm and, in proper Webster fashion, I had let the questions fly.

Me: "Do you DESERVE all that money?"

Him: "Ach, sometimes my Presbyterian guilt complex hangs HEAVY on my bloody back! I'm not really committed to the free enterprise system, yet I'm part of a commercially successful free enterprise station and I naturally demand my pound of FLESH!"

Me: "Would you say you make your money out of other people's MISERY?"

Him: "I do, yes—by HELPING them!"

Me: "What's your IMAGE, do you think?"

Him: "Basically straight, basically frank, a bit eccentric, a bit of a buffoon . . . a good reporter—and I'm scared witless of being thought a pompous BRAGGART!"

Me: "What's bad about the job?"

Him: "You DO lose some sensitivity. You DO tend to use people. It DESTROYS your patience with others. You feel a little bit isolated at times. . . ."

Me: "What's the use of your show?"

Him: "It gives all the immediacy of radio news. I cover spot stories and give depth newspapers haven't got space for. And Webster is AGIN the government. That's one function: To be AGIN the government! People like this kind of radio because they feel they can't be edited—you can't because it's live. There's a great goddam demand for this kind of participation."

Me: "Are you superficial?"

Him: "I'm accused of it. I flip from subject to subject to subject. I've GOT to! The worst that can happen is that I lose my audience—then I'm no BLOODY good at all!"

Me: "What do you hate most?"

Him: "LIARS!"

Me: "Who is the best in Canada in your work?"

Him: "Pierre Berton."

Me: "What do you think of these broadcasters—Gordon Sinclair, Pat Burns and Peter Gzowski?"

Him: "I've great respect for Sinclair. He's been rougher and ruder than I'll ever be. . . . I've got more of a sense of PROPRIETY! Burns was one of the best rabble-rousers in the EARLY days of hotlines. Gzowski does a nice, soft-sell interview and when he GROWS UP he'll be a good professional performer."

Me: "Who was the worst person you ever interviewed?"

Him: "Jack Benny—DULL!"

Me: "The hardest?"

Him: "Trudeau. Very gracious and gentle beforehand. But during the interview you BETTER be right! Coldblooded, very tough. When he calls you 'Sir' he's getting mad."

Me: "Funniest?"

Him: "Farley Mowat. He's the best bit of journalistic showbiz in the country!"

Me: "How's your French?"

Him: "I get by."

Me: "Why don't you learn it properly? You're always TALKING about Canadian unity . . . work it into the show some way."

Him: "Good idea. I WILL!"

Me: "I'm going to say that in the story . . . . Now, in 15 seconds, what would YOU say if you could talk back to Webster?"

Him: "You got no political GUTS, Webster! You've never nailed your flag to a mast. You EVADE! You sound like a socialist some days, other days like a SLEAZY liberal! What AR-R-RE you?"

Me: "Name one big defeat."

Him: "The CONTINUED success and victory of Social Credit!"

And on and on till the ferry slipped into the mainland wharf.

Ten seconds to go and Webster was winding up *City Mike*. He promised to be back on Monday, rattled off his phone numbers, shouted goodnight and quickly punched all the buttons on the switchboard. But phones kept ringing in the little studio. The union men shook hands and said goodbye. Webster put on his raincoat, then his hat. The phones kept on ringing, and no one answered. The phones were ringing as he shut off the lights. And we could hear them ringing as we walked down the hall.

9. So Many Will Die (1971)

CALCUTTA, INDIA—It's only beginning. In the next few months, as the rains fall, this corner of the world could see death on a scale men haven't recorded before. East Pakistan refugees, fleeing an army gone mad, continue swarming into India. The count at writing [late June] is seven million, take or leave a million—nobody *really* knows. By the end of July, the prediction was for 10 million. There may be famine and there may be bullets. But it's the rain, the experts say, that will do most of the killing. Torrents of it will come plunging down, about 100 inches in three months. Large portions of the land will be flooded. And when the water has fallen much of it will be still, and awful, deadly bacteria will breed.

Think of just this one problem: Say, amid all that water, India and the relief agencies manage somehow to feed the millions, give them medical care and shelter; where, though, where in God's name in all that high water and mud, will those men, women and children go to *the bathroom*? What good will the food and medicine and shelter be if these people—crammed into tarpaulin-covered barracks, grass huts and concrete sewer pipes—live knee-high in their own excrement? Right now there isn't an answer . . . the horror is just beginning.

Two weeks in West Bengal, one of three Indian states bordering East Pakistan, and that's my main conclusion. Two weeks of visiting refugee camps, hospitals and border points, talking with relief workers, Indian government people and soldiers, Bangladesh (what the freedom fighters now call East Pakistan) officials, and again and again there is the same thought: It's all just starting. I shot hundreds of pictures knowing many of the subjects wouldn't be living when this saw print, like the old man with folded hands [on the cover of the magazine where the article was first published]. His name was Hashbery Mondel and he used to own a small grocery store.

How old was he, I wanted to know.

"I am not so old," he answered through an interpreter, "that I will not be able to return to Bangladesh when it is free."

But he was wrong about that. He would be long dead.

In the air-conditioned Embassy Room of Calcutta's Grand Hotel, a big, sweating Australian drained the last of his gin and tonic. He was a reporter and had been out at the camps all day. He stared at himself in the mirror behind the bar.

"Pain is pain," he said to nobody in particular. "You can only write so *much* about pain . . . I'm cutting out."

So it was with many of the world's press. When the news broke of a cholera epidemic, dozens of them flew in. Cholera still has a dreadful magic. But the disease was brought under control fairly quickly. (Though it may break out again, of course.) Now what else was there to say about the refugees? Lots were coming in. Lots were dying. Lots told terribly similar stories of shootings, burnings and rapings. There was India's daily heroic effort of housing and feeding the hordes; the dedicated relief people working their hearts out; the continuing indifference of most of the world's governments; the United Nations' traditional paralysis; and so on. But none of it news, not anymore. So after about a week the newsmen started leaving. And none was sorry. The incredible heat, the stink and screaming poverty on the streets of Calcutta, the pathetic refugees in their camps where ditches already were filling with putrefying water . . . it was a good place to *leave*. The Grand grew quiet.

The reasons for all the death and destruction in East Pakistan, and the millions of refugees who have fled from there into India, are many and complex. There isn't space here to go into detail. Basically, however, this is what happened: Last December, free elections were held in Pakistan for a constituent assembly. The Awami League, led by Sheikh Mujibur Rahman, won by a majority. In part this was because the party is based in East Pakistan (separated from West Pakistan by a thousand miles of Indian territory) and 78 million of the nation's 130 million people live there. The League immediately put forward a demand for regional autonomy. Pakistan's military dictator, General Yahya Kahn—whose declared wish it was that the elections be held in the first place, with a view to returning the government to civilian control—decided, after some months of parleying, this was a move to secede. On March 25 he ordered his troops to crush it. A dreadful bloodbath—which continues—was visited upon East Pakistan. The millions of terrified refugees are testimony to it. Meanwhile, guerrilla cadres are fighting back at the army; Sheikh Mujibur is reportedly under house arrest in West Pakistan, and sick and starving refugees, many of whom who have walked for two weeks to get there, continue to cross into India at the rate of about 100,000 a day.

The world community has known all this for months—but the man-made disaster grows, and, probably, much worse is to come.

One night, though, the place did jump again a little, when 15 young English men and women checked in. They had chartered a plane, loaded it with three Land Rovers and some medical supplies. They had come to help the refugees, their leader announced. Do-gooders. Apparently they show up at every catastrophe. Bursting with good will and energy but generally useless; governments and relief agencies dread them.

What were their plans?

Well, two of them knew about well-digging, and . . . er . . . there must be *lots* of things. . . .

Why not leave the Land Rovers and supplies, suggested one relief worker—and get out!

They did, too. Next morning they happily bought two sitars, some Indian dresses and jewelry, and flew home.

However, one young do-gooder who came in much the same way stayed. Jillian Wellington, 20, from Ottawa, arrived in Calcutta the same day I did. She had been in another state on a scholarship learning Indian dancing. She had been on a train 2½ days and landed, barefoot and in a sari, at the Oxfam offices.

"I want to help," she told Oxfam's field director Raymond Cournoyer, of Magog, Quebec. There wasn't much need for dancers . . . but Raymond has a way with people. Many see him as the most effective relief worker in the area, and Oxfam as the most effective agency. His way is that he somehow inspires those working with him to grow a little bigger, to grow a bit beyond what they were before. He has the stuff of heroes and Canada can be proud of him.

In a few days, Jill, without secretarial skills, was operating at full steam around the office. Not romantic perhaps, but useful.

"Thank God it's not me!" is everyone's thought on their first visit to a camp. And it returns again and again. Nothing on earth justifies that much misery. Animals don't live like that—in the wet heat, 20,000 to 50,000 people live pressed together in their own stench, filth and noise, without privacy, along with a million flies. The statistics suddenly become flesh, blood, eyes, hair, teeth, and intelligence.

There, on a dry patch between tents, were three statistics—a mother and two babies. One of the babies showed no sign of life. Occasionally, the mother rolled it to one side and then the other; I don't know why. The other baby kept up a steady whimper. Its eyes were infected and a crust of pus had closed the left one. The mother waved flies off this baby's face when too many settled there. An hour later, the scene hadn't changed.

And statistics followed me and my cameras. Half a hundred stark-naked kids, handsome with big dark eyes, but with bellies too swollen, sores on their skins, and many with watering, inflamed eyes. Solemn kids, watching every move I made. I tried smiling but just got stares, though not unfriendly—what the hell was there to smile about? But then while loading, I dropped one of the cameras, and yes, thank God, *that* was funny. A lot of grins, a couple of giggles, one screech. And when—swearing—I bent down to pick it up—that was even funnier.

And the old woman, naked under a mud-caked sheet, lying in the shadow of the hospital tent, she was a statistic. Soon of the other sort though. The Indian doctor came outside and said she would maybe live another two hours. There wasn't anything to do but let her lie there where it was a bit cooler than inside. I leaned in very close with the camera and it took the longest time to focus. She looked straight into the lens, but surely didn't see a thing.

Women on their haunches cooking rice over little fires, women feeding babies, men just sitting and staring, a man and wife sitting cross-legged in a bamboo hut, yelling at each other, their faces contorted with anger—all statistics.

On the raised doorstep of another hut lay a baby with a banana leaf tucked under its head. The mother poured water from a kettle onto the baby's forehead. It had a fever and she was trying to keep its brain cool. The water ran down from the baby's forehead onto the banana leaf and from there into a pot. When the kettle was empty the mother filled it with the contents of the pot. Then she let the thin stream of water run onto the baby's head again. They were two more statistics. The mother's sari had loosened, baring her bosom. She fixed the sari when I approached but otherwise she seemed all alone with her child.

When we left the camp, a child wrapped in a green cloth lay in the grass by the roadside.

"What's that child doing there?" I asked my guide, D. Mukkerjee, a government press officer.

"It's dead," he said. "The truck hasn't had time to pick it up yet."

The half-hundred followers watched as I look pictures of the little corpse. They watched Mukkerjee and me climb into our car. But when I waved goodbye, they didn't wave back.

Mukkerjee had been taking reporters out to the camps for weeks. He is a frail, tired-looking, helpful, polite man who rarely speaks.

I remember him saying two things on different visits to camps:

"It was an accident these people were born human beings," he said. "They were born, they lived, and many will die here. But they never had the *taste* of life."

And: "When I take my meal comfortably in my home at night, all *this,"* and he waved his hand around the camp, "flashes through my mind."

One time a three-man French television team asked if they could follow us in their car so Mukkerjee could guide them as well. As the day wore on Mukkerjee grew even more silent than usual. Clearly he was upset. One reason was an incident that occurred at a border crossing about 80 miles northeast of Calcutta. The Indian border security guard, carrying a bamboo stick and a Luger strapped to his belt, showed us the path along which for two months hundreds of thousands of refugees had straggled into India. The day before, in fact, 18,000 had come along there. It was about one p.m., the hottest time of day, and the Frenchmen had lugged their cameras for half a mile. But the path was deserted. No refugees. The Frenchmen sweated in silence, but the border guard was disturbed.

"Gentlemen, I'm sorry," he said. "I'm really so very sorry, gentlemen, that there are no refugees. It must be too hot for them. I'm witness to thousands walking here—but now there are none. I am so *sorry!"*

He was also mad, he confessed later, because the French reporter never asked questions. The team moved fast into camps or hospitals; the reporter talked on camera; they shot some random film; and they were out again.

"How can they explain what it's like here without asking questions?" Mukkerjee demanded to know. He had a point. And, in one instance anyway, it cost the French a significant item.

Bongaon Hospital is about 60 miles north of Calcutta, 25 from the East Pakistan border. The man in charge, the always smiling Dr. P. R. De, said he had 234 patients but beds for only 68. And indeed the floors of the wards and hallways were packed with the sick. Groans, and little screams, and retching. Dr. De said smiling that he had 55 patients with cholera. Off the Frenchmen ran to the cholera ward. Dr. De rattled off more disease and death statistics. And then he said that in the past 45 days he had treated 163 bullet cases. That was interesting. Some people said refugees were exaggerating their tales of West Pakistan soldiers shooting unarmed civilians. So then Dr. De introduced me to nine-year-old Amina Khatun, a Moslem, shot in the leg on March 29. I met a boy, who would not give his name or age, who had his right arm shot off; a girl who got a bullet in the back and the only way to extract it was by cutting through her right breast; a young woman shot in the arm.

"War," explained Dr. De, smiling.

* * * * *

And war is what Hussain Ali talked about for two hours a few days later. Hussain Ali was deputy chief of the Pakistan high commission in Calcutta. When the Pakistan army attacked the city of Dacca on March 25, the diplomat raised the Bangladesh flag over the mission and pledged himself to the imprisoned leader Sheikh Mujibur Rahman. He now heads the as yet unrecognized nation's only foreign post.

"We are fighting back," he said. "We don't have many men yet, but so far we have killed 12,000 of the enemy and wounded 35,000.

"They have killed at least two million of us. Pakistan can never be one country again. Every family in the country has been affected by the slaughter. We will fight as long as necessary until Bangladesh is free."

Then he showed me some photographs of the corpses of women who had been raped to death.

"All my life I've been a diplomat—but now I fight," he said. "I know of one incident where they gathered four trucks full of women and girls. In front of the Continental Hotel in Dacca they made them get out. And then they raped them. One of the girls was 10.

"We will win!" said Hussain Ali. "We're getting reports that the army doesn't venture out after dark any more. They are getting scared. Our boys in the villages are so motivated. They say: 'Give us guns!'

"The horror stories are many," he said. "My wife and I adopted an 11-year-old girl who had seen all her family killed. But we had to put her into a mental hospital. At first she couldn't speak at all. And then she began to say over and over again: "Father, father, why have they cut you? Why do they put salt and pepper on the wound?"

Hussain Ali told me to tell this to Canadians:

"Canada is a friendly and humane country. It has often taken the lead in the United Nations. It's a great democracy. You're the only country we know that has almost unrestricted immigration of colored people. My appeal is that we are a nation of 75 million people who are fighting for an independence that's been forced upon us. There's no going back for us. Canada should come forward and recognize this and give us moral and material help. The Canadian people would earn our everlasting gratitude."

While flocks of Calcutta's sinister hooded crows cawed ceaselessly in the courtyard, I talked to others in the Bangladesh mission: a politician, a soldier, a doctor, a stenographer, a businessman, and a journalist. They asked not to have their names used or pictures taken. Their wives and children were still in East Pakistan and they feared retaliation. "Although under the circumstances," one said, "I've forfeited the right to think of my family."

The men said many of the same things as Hussain Ali. One mentioned he understood the shooting and burning—"You expect the enemy to kill, not kiss you"—but not the raping. Another said that the prime target of the guerrillas now was not so much the Pakistan army as the "Quislings," the collaborators, among their own people. A third noted that nothing was known of the millions affected by the cyclone last November. He said that certainly the food and medicine the world had shipped in was never distributed. "There's no rational reason," he said, "to suppose that anyone has survived."

The journalist said:

"Our ultimate aim is to return to a free Bangladesh. It may be a long war. We look at it as them killing human beings, and us killing beasts."

That night in Oxfam headquarters—two shabbily furnished rooms in a little hotel—some of the organization's volunteer young Indian doctors gathered. Three of them were women. They spend all their days in the camps or organizing other volunteers to go.

"I've never been more disillusioned with the whole structure of the international community, with the United Nations, with the Commonwealth," one of them said.

"And so will you by the time you leave," added another.

True enough. The indifference of governments and people—including us in Canada—or the slowness of their token gestures in money and words, are hard to understand. Standing in the rain in one of the human garbage dumps that dot the lush land around Calcutta, it's *beyond* comprehension.

These places shouldn't be.

This war, these refugees, if only because of the incredible numbers of people involved, are the world's responsibility. The pressure on India, itself poor, is growing unbearable. God knows what may have happened by the time this is published. Calcutta, always turbulent, has reached the boiling point. Political assassinations are the order of the day. Nobody knows how many people live in that city, maybe eight million, maybe 12 million. It's certain that thousands of refugees have already entered and more continue to come. The city can't stand it. If new refugees find no shelter in the lashing rain, as experts fear, they may march on villages and towns, indeed Calcutta, and take shelter by force. I and other reporters observed lots of Indian troops dug in around the East Pakistan border. Will India go to war? And what *then* of the refugees? India can't take care of them as well as fight. And would West Pakistan's good friend China join such a war? And if China, who else? So speculation rages now.

A Calcutta steel merchant, whose family had lived there for generations, told me one night: "I'm thinking of taking my wife and children and getting out. Life has always been cheap here, but *now*. . . . We're going crazy. Soon we will all be fighting each other in the streets. *You'll see!*"

And so back to the calm Raymond Cournoyer who *doesn't* talk like that. He is too busy thinking about latrines. The problem of the disposal of human excrement in the camps must be solved. It is at the centre of the storm which will come anyway, but maybe then less severely. Raymond and his Oxfam people, the other relief agency people and the Indian government are wracking their brains over it.

Raymond has other things on his mind as well: organizing sanitation, medical and food distribution teams; providing medicine, milk and protein foods for kids, shelter and ground sheets, clothing, soap. Right now, he said, he was planning ahead till the end of August. After that it might be more useful to concentrate on a single program, feeding kids for instance.

"Tell them at home," he said, "that there's absolutely no overlapping of work among the agencies."

"Oh yes, and tell them, please," said Raymond, "that the money they give goes to help the *refugees*. Make sure they know—it goes to the *refugees*."

10. Ninety Seconds of Daylight (1971)

FAIR WARNING: This may not be your cup of tea; the question raised may not seem important, interesting, or even relevant, or maybe you've already got enough problems of your own. On the other hand. . . .

Recently I visited a hog-producing outfit in British Columbia, a cattle feedlot and a similar operation for sheep in Alberta, and a chicken and egg enterprise in Ontario. The trip was an eye opener. Producing meat and eggs has become very sophisticated, specialized, big business in Canada. And the word is these trends will accelerate. It all depends on the market and the market is us and we go right on multiplying. Besides, we could be eating lots more meat, like the Americans do—about 50 more pounds per person, per year than Canada's per capita figure of 188.5 pounds per year.

The four operations were big and among the most advanced, technologically, in the country. Their names don't matter as others in the business work in similar ways, or would like to. The four, you see, are also very profitable.

The idea was to get some notion of the intensive "farming" of animals in Canada. And just that was achieved—some notion; I didn't become an instant expert. Nowadays, raising steers or pigs to market weight, *quickly,* is a complex affair. Years of experience, a *dozen* sciences, and much business know-how are required. One thing soon learned, though, was that "farming," as the word is generally understood, was altogether inappropriate.

What I saw was *manufacturing.* They were *factories* where, in a closely controlled environment, on a tight schedule, using much automation, meat and eggs were produced, 24 hours a day, 365 days a year. And the people running them didn't call themselves farmers. Managers, factory workers—but not farmers. They agreed their operations were factories, although *they* didn't like the name.

Factories then, but with a difference—the product lives. Not particularly happy places to visit either. They showed man's wonderful ingenuity, but also his total power over other living things and his disdain for them. What was made there was for eating. The animals—thousands of them—were fed, watered, treated medically, and housed according to rigid formulas designed with just one thing in mind: efficiency. An efficient animal—one which at minimum cost grows large, fat and edible in a minimum of time—is a profitable animal. And that's what it's all about: profits. All advertising to producers, for instance, emphasizes profits. A beast's comfort or natural inclinations are considered only in the light of efficiency. "Pleasure" isn't a factor at all.

Intensive livestock production is here to stay, and for good reasons: low retail prices; improved disease control; uniform quality (though not necessarily better quality); reasonable returns for the producer; and animal protein gets to the mass of people.

There are also some drawbacks: Chemicals and drugs are used which could enter our food as residue in meat, milk and eggs (e.g., the hormone diethylstilbestrol, which reportedly is appearing in U.S. beef livers in increasing amounts); and the animals could develop behavioral and psychological abnormalities due to confinement, crowding, or lack of comfort. Dr. Franklin Loew, of the department of veterinary physiology at the University of Saskatchewan, told meetings of Canadian Humane Societies recently that "these areas have received practically no study by experts." In other words, we're doing great in our production of massive amounts of meat and eggs, but don't care much about their quality or what effects our techniques are having on the animals.

Dr. Loew, one of the few in Canada who has spoken out on the subject, also said that many agriculturists claim that as long as production increases an animal must be all right; that a suffering or uncomfortable animal simply wouldn't gain weight, give milk or lay eggs. But then Loew quoted animal behaviourist Professor W.H. Thorpe of Cambridge University: "High productivity is not reliable evidence for the absence of severe stress."

Thorpe has also written: "Confinement, just because it restricts what is both physiologically and ethologically one of the most basic and all-pervading activities of animals, namely the locomotory responses, is most powerful in its effects."

At the pig plant in British Columbia there was much concern about stress in the animals. Every effort was made to minimize it. There was so little action in the lives of the hogs, one of the men there told me, that even a little excitement could occasionally cause one to topple over dead from a heart attack, or just lie down and not move for three days.

Other items learned from him:

- Housed in the gray, low-slung, windowless, steel-and-concrete, heated, ventilated and very clean barns, the pigs see from birth to their date at the slaughterhouse approximately 90 seconds of daylight.
- Yes, he ate "quite a bit of bacon."
- Pigs are curious, intelligent animals—"Any pig here has got Lassie beat to hell."
- Feeding, watering and dung removal was all automatic.
- In four years the place would be operating 100 percent on artificial insemination. They'd get along then with 60 percent less boars—one

ejaculation fertilizes 12 to 15 sows.

- No, the animals didn't have much pleasure as such. Experimentation was going on with dummy sows for piglets to feed from so the mother can get started faster on her next litter; so also with dummy sows to coax boars to give their semen. Dutch researchers have developed an apparatus whereby a pig can be trained to dung on order by giving it "a certain sensory stimulation" as it stands feeding.
- Animals are handled as little as possible—to avoid stress.
- Pigs don't understand doors. If you opened them they wouldn't stray very far, if at all—"These pens are their world."
- "If you threw a little rock in one of these pens they would play with it for hours."

In the cattle and sheep feedlots in Alberta, the animals were at least outside in the fresh air. But the pens are crowded, dusty when it's dry, muddy when wet, and deep in manure; in summer incredible numbers of flies gather, in winter it gets very cold. And, of course, the animals never see green grass.

An article in a recent *Journal* of *Animal Science* says: "Very little is known about the social or psychological factors that may be important in the grouping of cattle in pens to finish them for market. Such factors as group size and pecking order are *known* to be important for other species, but it is only *assumed* they are for cattle."

The Ontario chickens also lived in a windowless, totally controlled environment. Triple-decked rows and rows of wire cages stuffed with softly cackling, eating, egg-laying hens. The building measured 332 by 34 feet and held 29,760 of them. The cages were 15 by 18 inches and each contained five birds. The unit was entirely automated and it took one man less than a working day to operate.

Lights stimulate production, so when the birds first come in, at 20 weeks, the place is lit 10 hours a day. By the time they are shipped off to the soupmaker—14 months and 20 dozen eggs per bird later—the lights are burning 18 hours a day. To prevent too much damage from pecking, the owner told me, beaks are blunted and combs and wattles trimmed. He, too, noted the importance of limiting stress.

If stress worries stockmen so much, it might be asked, why haven't they tried removing some of the actual sources of it—the eyes, ears and maybe vocal cords of their animals? What use are these organs now anyway? Would the animals taste any different?

Public concern about intensive livestock production began in England in 1964 with a book called *Animal Machines* by Ruth Harrison. So far, it seems, the British have remained the only ones to get worked up about the issue. Apparently few of the practices Mrs. Harrison attacked are in use in Canada. But there are two: battery raising of chickens in cages, and the tethering of swine, i.e. pregnant sows. Shortly after the book came out, the British government set up a committee to investigate its charges. The committee's eventual report said: "We accept that although pain, suffering, and stress are certainly not identical in animals and men, there are sound reasons for believing they are substantial in domestic animals and that there is no justification for disregarding them." Some of the committee's findings were:

- Every animal should have sufficient freedom of movement to get up, lie down, groom normally, turn around, and stretch its limbs.
- Facilities should be provided to train stockmen in the operation of intensive husbandry units.
- Minimum sizes and types of cages and stalls should be set by law for poultry, pigs and cattle.
- De-beaking should be eliminated and trimming combs and wattles (dubbing) should be prohibited in birds over five days old.

Around the same time an opinion poll in England showed:

	% agreed	
	Farmers	Public
Freedom for all animals to turn around in their stalls	85%	87%
Poultry to have room to spread wings	78%	91%
Cattle and sheep to have access to the open for some part of the day in fair weather	76%	80%

Dr. Loew said in his little-noted speech: "Intensive livestock production provides many benefits, and in Canada, appears apparently not to have been abused to the extent that it had been in England." Are we then more humanitarian than the British? Not likely. Or are we just less up-to-date technologically? As a layman there was no way of telling by looking at the pigs, sheep, cattle and chickens. There was the uncomfortable impression, however, that they weren't so much living as *existing*. It wasn't really a thrill to learn where one's meals were coming from, and I suspect a lot of people would have felt the same way. I also suspect that if anyone tried to raise cats, dogs, elephants, tigers, grizzly bears or hawks by these methods, there would be riots in the streets.

Dr. Loew made two recommendations:

1. The federal department of agriculture should increase the use of the services of trained animal behaviorists in conducting research into the behavioural effects of intensive husbandry, particularly in swine and chickens.

2. Everybody involved with intensive livestock production—architects, agriculturists, veterinarians, engineers, animal behaviourists, representatives from consumer groups, etc.—should be brought together to study the subject.

Dr. Loew said that in Canada we should concern ourselves with two main questions:

To the producer: Is production the sole criterion by which a farming practice can be justified?

To the public: Could you, would you, pay the higher food price which would result from lessening the intensity of livestock production?

An Englishman named John Lawrence (1753–1839) put it in another, less cryptic, way. Described as a "literary farmer," he was an authority on agriculture and management of domestic animals.

> Justice, in which are included mercy, or compassion, obviously refers to sense and feeling. How is the essence of justice divisible? Can there be one kind of justice for men, and another for brutes? Or is feeling in them a different thing to what it is in ourselves? Is not a beast produced by the same rule, and in the same order of generation with ourselves? Is not his body nourished by the same food, hurt by the same injuries; his mind actuated by the same passions and affections which animate the human breast; and does not he, also, at last, mingle his dust with ours, and in like manner surrender up the vital spark to the aggregate, or fountain of intelligence? Is this spark, or soul, to perish because it chanced to belong to a beast? Is it to become annihilate? Tell me, learned philosophers, how that may possibly happen?

And that's the question.

11. Nigeria: A Time to Heal (1972)

ENUGU, NIGERIA—"You should have come sooner," said Tilus Eluwah, my driver, the first day we set out. His hands gripped the wheel of the rickety Citroen, his eyes never left the narrow highway. It was tricky driving on that ripped and shell-pocked road. The holes were full of water and you couldn't tell their depth. We hadn't spoken for an hour. All the windows were open but it didn't help much in the sodden heat. The road wound through yam fields and black-green patches of jungle. Traffic—as everywhere in Nigeria—hogged the centre of the road, swerving only at the last second to pass. A fearful game of chicken that often ended in death. Titus and I sweated a lot on the road, but rarely conversed. Anyhow, he wasn't much of a talker, or much for giving out opinions. But there it was, unasked for: "You should have come sooner." And he was absolutely right.

I should have come sooner. The whole world should have come sooner.

Remember Biafra? A Canadian diplomat in Nigeria told me we are on record at External Affairs as getting more emotionally involved with that bit of Africa—the bloody, 30-month-long war that raged there—than with any other foreign affair in our history.

Remember the television films, the newspaper stories? No civil war was ever so publicized. Sometimes for weeks on end it hit us every day. We squirmed, sighed, wrote angry letters and gave money. Preachers begged, Stanley Burke scolded, and in Ottawa they said as little as possible.

The reports we got were of black men killing black men, and of their cool, articulate leaders explaining why, but most of all of starving children. The pictures—swollen bellies, protruding ribs, thin sticks for limbs, and huge, dull eyes. Sometimes it got too horrible; the guilt cut too deep.

The war ended more than two-and-a-half years ago on January 15, 1970. But in that time something remarkable happened. And nobody told us. It was good news, too. . . .

Perhaps a kind of miracle.

It took place—and that's what should be kept in mind—in an African country, independent only a dozen years, described by one of its own as ". . . a mere geographical expression. At best an agglomeration of tribal nations . . . with as much difference between them as between Germans, Russians and Turks." A country 10,000 square miles smaller than British Columbia but with three times Canada's population, made up of 200 different tribes speaking as many languages. A country with poor communications, severe unemployment, much complaint of corruption in government, and highways deserted after dark for fear of armed robbers. A so-called underdeveloped country. That's where it happened . . . and the conclusion is that if we look back on our own wars, then we have no record of an aftermath so relatively bloodless as this one. Nor any record of such a concerted effort, with very little outside help, to rehabilitate, forgive, and forget.

What the world feared—and what petrified those living there—was that at war's end there would be a blood bath. Particularly, the Ibos, the dominant tribe, would suffer. Federal troops would massacre them.

It didn't happen. There were isolated incidents of gratuitous killing—it had been a bitter war—and there were reports of federal soldiers looting and raping. But there were no large-scale reprisals. That hideous word "genocide," bandied about throughout the war, was a lie.

Following the peace, thousands still died of starvation and lack of medical attention but misleading predictions, and even reports, had this occurring by the *millions*. (The war's total death toll is estimated at about one million—the exact figure will never be known.)

Biafran soldiers were told to lay down their arms and return to their villages. So also the hundreds of thousands of refugees hiding in the bush. There was no rejoicing in Nigeria following the victory. What most people felt was simply an immense sense of relief. The head of state, General Yakubu Gowon, told his army no medals would be struck for this campaign. He called it a war of "no victors and no vanquished." He decreed three days of national prayer. It was now time, he said, for "binding up the nation's wounds."

I spent some days in Lagos, Nigeria's capital, and travelled through a large part of what was Biafra. From what I saw, and from what I learned from dozens of people on both sides, and whites who had lived in Nigeria since the war, that is exactly what government and people have striven for.

It says something about the incredible pace of change in a country like Nigeria that most people didn't really want to talk about the war. Some, undoubtedly, because they didn't like being reported. But most, I felt, because it was over and done with. Today and tomorrow were interesting, yesterday less so.

A number of Ibos told me they had experienced job discrimination, but not one claimed it was policy anywhere. There are pockets of starvation in the East, but I was told this occurred in pre-war days as well, and was usually due to natural phenomena such as a bad harvest. Agriculture, I learned, had in fact recovered almost completely. In general, prosperity was about equal to that of the rest of Nigeria.

All this has been happening over the last two-and-a-half years.

OKIGWI—The area that was Biafra (Nigeria's East Central, South Eastern and Rivers States) still bears the marks of the civil war: walls dotted with the tiny craters bullets make; shelled buildings; few intact bridges in a land laced with streams and rivers; damaged roads; and the war's most awful legacy, the maimed. The area holds at least 20,000 amputees. In that part of the world the common lot of cripples is to become beggars. I was told that Hopeville Rehabilitation Centre, about 70 miles south of Enugu, East Central State's capital, was the most effective operation of its kind. Started almost immediately after the war, it is run by two Marist Brothers, Francis, an Irishman, and James, a Texan. Some 220 amputees at a time find a temporary home there and, indeed, hope. They are fitted with, and taught to maneuver, whichever limb is missing and meanwhile can learn a trade.

Energetic though haggard looking, Brother Francis told me that at first artificial limbs were imported, costing from $135 to $225. But then about a year ago, a 23-year-old physiotherapist and CUSO worker, Janet Gainer of Edmonton, arrived and developed a leg, which the amputees could carve themselves from wood and other materials found locally, at a cost of $21 to $30. Other skills or trades they could learn included welding, carpentry, tailoring, leather work and the operation of a poultry farm, piggery, rabbitry, bakery or fishery.

One important condition is that a Hopeville-trained man pass on what he's learned to another amputee free of charge. The centre has set up 10 other such co-operatives in the state. The principle is simple: get the people working and the operation perpetuates itself. At first some portion of the harvest or income is returned as payment to Hopeville which then invests it in still another setup. Money, of course, said Brother Francis, is the key to getting the schemes off the ground in the first place and working on any kind of scale. A fishery costs $1,500, a bakery $6,000.

At one point Brother Francis stopped to talk with a small woman in rags carrying a baby boy. She was a widow, had no one to care for her and had come to the centre for help. She and the child suffered *kwashiorkor*. The boy's swollen belly, legs and ankles were one of the war's familiar sights.

"I didn't care who won it," Brother Francis said. "I just wanted the bloody thing to stop!"

He stroked the child's legs. "We put hundreds like him in the ground."

Later, Brother Francis showed me the cemetery, a field grown high with razor-sharp grass. He said they had lost count during the war but guessed at least 400 children were buried there.

"It was gruesome, gruesome . . ." he muttered.

UYO—A Nigerian told me of Jack Pearpont, 26: "He is the best Canadian here. (There are about 1,000.) If this was Britain we would elect him to Parliament."

Lean and freckled, Pearpont, of Saskatoon, sports a reddish beard. He is quiet and sure of himself. He has an intense dislike for ostentation, yet often wears a tie in that ungodly climate because he deals a lot with Nigerian headmasters and knows they appreciate it.

Pearpont worked two years for CUSO (Canadian University Service Overseas) in Ghana, followed by two years as CUSO co-ordinator in eastern Nigeria, and is now running a unique CUSO/Canadian International Development Aid project, which is "so simple it's ridiculous." Elsewhere I heard that, though not big, it was one of Canada's most effective aid programs ever.

During the war, both sides used schools as barracks and soldiers burned most of the furniture for firewood. There was thus a dire need for desks. With about $1,000,000 in Canadian money, the program has injected cash into local communities—where it's needed most—by using their materials and labour to build new desks under the supervision of headmasters and school committees. Pearpont said the project was nearing completion and that of the roughly 1,000 schools serviced—involving some 1,000 people on school committees and perhaps 8,000 carpenters—there had been only one case of money mismanagement.

"It's a miracle," he said.

Most agencies, of course, love to put emblems or initials on whatever they supply. When the desks are finished, Pearpont said, headmasters ask if he would like to paste on a maple leaf to show who paid for them. "But we say, 'No, it's your work, your organization—so they're *your* desks.' Then they see we really mean it."

I watched Pearpont in a shirt dark with sweat but wearing his tie, explain administrative procedures to a room full of elderly headmasters. In the long run, he told me, acquiring that basic administrative know-how might be more important than the material benefits.

Pearpont suffers bouts of malaria—"So bad I want to do away with myself"—and I asked him why he stayed on in Nigeria.

"I'm not impressed by Canadian materialism," he said. "Here I'm working with people and what I'm doing, I think, is a good thing, I'm getting feedback. It's relevant."

ARO—It was a pity the rainy season's clouds hid the moon. It would have been perfect shining down on the circle of dancing, sweating, shouting men. The yellow eyes of a half-dozen oil lamps showed only flashes of them. And you could hardly see the drummers, the men hammering the wooden xylophone, the clusters of other villagers watching. Just once the clouds might have parted, but they didn't. The moon never showed its face. A pity. It was a night to remember.

A few days earlier, 70-odd miles north, that same moon had stood over Enugu, capital of Nigeria's East Central State and once of dead Biafra, and lit up foxtrotters on the terrace of the Presidential Hotel. But that night didn't compare with the one in Aro. A companion recognized some of the well-dressed men and women on the floor. They belonged to eastern Nigeria's elite. People of money and position. People of influence before, during and after the Biafran war. People whose continuous, obvious well-being contrasted sharply with the condition of most of their countrymen.

To gain some notion of the aftermath of the well-publicized, 30-month civil war—there had been almost no news since it ended in January, 1970—I talked with such people, but it wasn't very satisfying or useful. With few exceptions, the conflict seemed hardly to have touched them. They were rarely the ones who had done the fighting, dying or suffering. And it was the latter, particularly, with whom we in Canada had been concerned.

The people the war bankrupted, widowed, orphaned, starved, maimed and killed were, of course, the so-called little people.

All day long clouds packed the sky. There was no wind. Nothing moved among the trees and climbers. Some people worked their plots of yams, but not many. It was better to sit very still in the dark, earthen-walled huts; maybe sip a little freshly tapped palm wine. Towards midday the air got so heavy it was like breathing warm water. Only the jungle's trillion insects exerted themselves.

Yet, around 4 p.m., people started coming out of their tiny homes, scattered willy-nilly about the bush, and making their way to the village's centre, an open, swept space ringed by big trees. First children, then men, then women.

Chief Simeon Amaobi Okorie, 31, had shown me around during the day. He was unusually young to be chief. An Ibo, the majority tribe in Biafra, he had commanded a battalion during the war and been wounded nine times. His village's principal industry was weaving palm-leaf mats; his people numbered 800 and their land, 60 square miles. From October, 1968, there had been almost constant fighting in the area. Okorie's people had fled deep into the bush where more than 60 died. The roofs of most homes had been destroyed or, if made of zinc, stolen. Rain had washed away the walls. Okorie's own house had been exactly one day old when he was called to service. He kept the blueprints as a memento. Reluctantly, he showed me the thatch-roofed hut he lived in. It wasn't finished and had no proper bedroom yet. Inside, it was bare except for a few pieces of homemade furniture. The roof would not keep out a heavy rain.

"To look at me, would you say I am a man without a zinc roof?" Okorie had asked, laughing.

No, you wouldn't. Slight, wiry and bearded, he walked with his back very straight. He was a cheerful man who liked to laugh. But there was no mistaking his authority. He might joke with the villagers but *he* took that initiative, not they.

The tour done, I had asked whether I might stay on, maybe even spend the night, to get to know the village a little better. He seemed surprised but said I should come back to check around 4 p.m.

Okorie was waiting in the open space in freshly pressed trousers and a clean, starched shirt.

"You will stay," he announced. "You will eat here tonight, sleep here—and we will dance!"

Then he sent some boys to fetch chairs.

"I have asked the old men," said the chief, "and they say no white man has ever slept here before. Not in the whole district of Uturu.

"We are grateful," he added, incredibly making *me* feel like the generous one. I didn't know how to top that bit of graciousness.

I met the elders then. Grey-haired distinguished-looking men, whose gentle handshakes sometimes lasted minutes and were released with small finger-snaps. The first, a very tall man with a wisp of grey on his upper lip, was treated with much respect by the others. Later, he would show me the compound he shared with his sons. We wouldn't see much because it would be dark. By flashlight he would offer a segment of a cola nut—which is always served on entering a home and is almost obligatory to accept—and I would break a tooth.

Drummers and the three men who played the xylophone settled in the centre of the open space. A few tentative taps, as small children formed a circle around them, and without further preliminaries they broke into a fast beat.

The kids instantly started shaking and jumping, moving all of themselves, around and around, faces tight with concentration. Several men kept pace with them shouting instructions, cheering them on. They stayed with them for nearly three hours, stuffing hunks of bread into the youngsters' mouths as they got hungry. Outside the circle stood other men and children, and behind them the women. Several hundred people all together. From those first taps, the musicians never stopped till midnight. As the night wore on others fed them bread, water, palm wine and cigarettes. Sometimes one might wipe away sweat with a small towel, but he would use only one hand while the other pounded on. Dancing started as the drums' volume and tempo increased and ended as they eased up.

The elders, the chief and I sat in a semicircle on chairs and small stools. I had given Okorie a bottle of whisky. He poured a shot glass full.

"I must drink first," he said. "I am chief."

He took a small taste.

"It's from overseas. Excellent!"

Then gulped down the rest.

My turn next and I did the same. And so it went around the circle until the bottle was empty.

"Now you must try Biafra gin," said the chief.

I had learned this was palm wine several days old, extremely potent and best consumed with care.

"In a cold land like yours," said Okorie, "you must need this. We will send it to you. We will keep you supplied."

One of the elders said this would be difficult because of Customs. There followed considerable discussion on the issue with about 10 others joining in.

A bit later our group was served several quart bottles of beer. No one had an opener, so the chief lifted the caps with his teeth. "That's how we did it in the army." The beer was warm.

Around 7 p.m., in the tropics' sudden way, it grew dark. People ran around yelling for oil lamps. The drums kept going. Night signalled the end of dancing for the children, and the men took over. Many had discarded their shirts and changed trousers for sarong-like affairs wrapped tightly above the knees and knotted about the waist. Some wore anklets of jiggling bits of bone. They wore no shoes.

The mood began to change. There was less laughing. The drumming was thicker, faster; dances lasted longer. They moved much as the youngsters had, but the hard thumping of big feet made still another drum. Each worked his body very like the next, but the force differed with a man's strength. And each seemed to use all he had. As a dance reached its climax, the lunging, heaving men seemed locked in battle with unseen foes. They snorted, grunted and shouted. It looked downright dangerous to approach the glistening bodies too closely. Indeed, two men with twigs kept onlookers back from the circle; which didn't prevent the occasional kid from leaping in and being whipped out again. Electricity sparked off the dancers and touched all in the blackness beneath the trees. The shadows throbbed, everybody was moving. Tension reached a pitch that tugged at your thinking. Then the drums would ease and so, gradually, the excitement. Crickets got a chance to be heard; women handed the dancers small towels; pots of palm wine did the rounds.

It was strictly a dance for the men but once an old woman couldn't stand it any longer and jumped in. She did a thing of her very own. There was much laughter. Nobody minded because she was old.

At about 8 p.m., the chief invited me to his home for food—rice and peppery chicken stew. It had been prepared by another man's wife because he wasn't married—"Not yet." I wanted to ask about the stew but didn't. Food isn't a subject men discuss.

The noise at the party had prohibited conversation; besides the chief had been dancing a lot himself. I had asked him earlier about the war and, in a vein similar to many others, he had said:

"Many died, but it is over. Personally, I think we should forget it, work hard, and make our lives normal again."

Rinsing his fingers in a bowl of water he said:

"In the war, when my people went in the bush they ate only cassava root. Many children died of *kwashiorkor* [extreme protein deficiency].

"You saw today that everything was destroyed here. Now it is getting better, but slowly. It takes much work. It takes money.

"We have enough land, but not enough money to farm it properly. We can supply labour, but money, my friend, is everything. . . . We don't want very much—just the help of God.

"Regarding myself, I worked hard and got secondary schooling. Once I was a police inspector. I have been to Ghana and Leopoldville. . . . But if I left here and took a good job somewhere, who would manage my people?"

We could hear the shouts of the dancers. The chief smiled.

"We forget the war when we dance," he said. "That is the Biafran way. Ah no, we cannot forget that name . . . Biafra!"

When we returned, the chief entered the circle between dances and made a speech lasting 20 minutes. God was mentioned often, and so were Jesus and Moses. When he was done, the men applauded and shouted, "Yaa! Yaa! Yaa!"

Okorie had given several such speeches, as had some of the elders. "It gives the dancers strength," he explained.

The drums picked up speed again. And the chief said to me:

"Now you dance."

I'd been told that whenever a Nigerian recommended something, one should at least try it. As it was, I was probably making enough social errors, without adding an outright refusal. Also, Okorie was the chief.

Up close, that wild, rotating dancing machine looked fearsome. Then suddenly I was part of it. But it wasn't so bad. The drums soon enough took over. I fought my invisible enemy as hard as the others. I could hear women and children screaming with laughter. No doubt I looked silly, but I was too deep in battle. When the drums finally slowed, I was trembling and sweat was running into my eyes. But I hadn't felt so good in a long time. Fellow dancers slapped my shoulders. The chief said, "You're hard to beat!" A cup of Biafra gin was thrust in my hand. And hopping towards me, knees out like a frog, came the number one elder, one hand behind his back. Someone gave me a shove and I was hopping towards him. When we met he gave me a hard hug. Then the hidden hand swung out, holding a present of an upside-down, angry chicken. My turn, obviously, to give a speech. Okorie translated. God occurred again, and so did Jesus and Moses. It lasted a quarter of an hour. All I said was: "Thank you for letting me stay in your village. It is a privilege. Your dancing is hard work. When my head is all white on top I will remember this night. Thank you."

I asked the chief if women were going to dance. Not that night, he said, but they would next morning. Regrettably, they never did and no wonder: their working day started at 4:30.

As the night went on, young men came over, shook hands, and stayed to chat. Three, in particular, said things that seem typical. They were not requests, simply statements.

Andrew, 19: "I would just like to finish my secondary schooling. It was interrupted by the war. I'm not going to school now because of lack of money, so I have to make farm work. All I want is to go back to school."

Jonathan, 26: "Prior to the war I was a trainee in mechanics and driving. Then I had to go into the army. I have three children, and when I came out there was nothing to feed them. Now I am a petty farmer and will stay that way because it takes money to change. I have no money."

Sylvester, 25: "I was a trader before the war—my own man. Now must help my father on his farm to feed the family. It will not change. . . . Right after the war people helped through feeding. Now we need financial help. We pray to

God to bring His grace to us."

A little before midnight, the drumming slowed and came to a stop—it was all over. People yawned, shouted goodnights, and wandered away into the dark. Within minutes the open space was empty. People sounds died away. The insects' steady whine took over, occasionally pierced by the scream of a night bird.

Okorie and I made our way to a one-room hut some distance from his own. It held two cots, a table and a bench; small lizards clung to the walls. The chief stripped down to bright red shorts and hung his clothes from a nail in the ceiling. He had danced and drunk as much as most, and looked tired. He flopped down on one of the cots and put his hands under his head.

"I want to tell you something," he said. "I want nothing for myself . . . only for my people."

He smiled then, and turning on his side murmured:

"Tonight has been the most Christmas we've enjoyed in three months."

12. Banana, Glue, Rubberface and Eight Other Canadians: The Men behind Sonny and Cher (1973)

HOLLYWOOD—"They're groovy," said the beautiful Cher Bono. She yawned then, exposing magnificent teeth. She wore a pale blue silk housecoat and sat with her legs up on the couch in her dressing room. Slumped next to her, smoking a cigar, Sonny Bono, her husband, said nothing.

The famous couple was pooped. That Saturday night they had finished taping the Christmas edition of the *Sonny and Cher Comedy Hour*. Work had started at 7 in the morning and now it was close to 11. For the stars, around whom all action revolved, it had been a hard day, as had the preceding five days of rehearsals. Songs, skits, one-liners, intros, dances, repeated over and over and over again. Tedious yet tense work, set to cruel deadlines. Exorbitant effort, it seemed at times, for 50-odd minutes of musical merriment.

Cher also had the flu, and had been up most of the previous night with Chastity, their four-year-old daughter, who had it as well. The Bonos' eyes drooped. They wanted to go home. Monday the crazy routine would start all over again.

But they had promised the interview.... Cher would do the talking, her large, luminous eyes staring ahead and seeing a hot bath.

"They're groovy" had referred to the 11 men from Canada who each play a key role in the show. Indeed, they are the ones who make it go. Without them, the enormously popular production would not be.

They were not there by accident. They had made it in big-time American television—as have dozens of others from Canada—because of talent, hard work, and because Canada had been a splendid training ground.

I'd watched them in action that week. I'd learned a little about them, though very little, absorbed as they were in their insulated, frantically competitive world. They had had little time, and no excessive interest, in talking to somebody from home. This had a lot to do with the production's terrible tempo and the pressure of the vast amounts of money involved, but also—what was there to say? Their life and work was in the United States, not in Canada anymore.

"Groovy." The word just hung there. The Bonos' retinue of maids and managers wandered about, fussing with costumes, makeup and wigs. The stars sat very still like tired children. Cher fiddled with one of her blood-red, very long fingernails.

I didn't really know what next to ask those rich, glamorous people. All week long I'd been asked, "Wanna meet Sonny and Cher?" but I had kept postponing it. I'd watched them, enjoyed them, admired their style and stamina—but what in the world could you say to them?

"What's it like working with all those Canadians?"

I'd tried that on the guest star, the massive William Conrad. (He plays the private detective in *Cannon.*)

"Canadians, Americans—what's the difference?" he'd growled. "They're pros!"

S & C were bound to say the same thing, and did, roughly—"Groovy".

Then another reason developed for staying away. The 11 from Canada had proven difficult to pin down all right. Bits of data and quotes had to be gathered from them on the run. So, finally, the only thing left that I could control was not to meet the stars. This silliness I nurtured all week.

But there we were, the three of us, in the dressing room, and I was in charge . . . and Art Fisher burst in. Always preoccupied and tense, he is the show's director and has won an Emmy for it. On the first day someone explained my presence to him as, "He's doing a thing on the Canadians."

Without looking up from his script, Fisher had muttered, "That's his problem."

"You really sang tonight, man!" he said to Cher. "Sensational! Dynamite!" And he ran out again.

But it provided the break to swiftly think up 11 penetrating questions. The interview then galloped along.

Q: "What do you think of Danny Mann, Cher?"

A: "He's my joy."

As production assistant, Danny, 24, co-ordinates, on instructions from the producers and director, the complex process that is a TV variety show. It's the best spot to learn the business. It involves remembering a million details, running a lot, and yet always being at the big guys' beck and call. The son of actor Larry Mann, Danny could think of no drawback to his job—"Except if you can't take the chew-outs." His qualifications include a degree in theatre arts, specializing in television, and being driver and go-fer of Norman Jewison (also Canadian) when the latter was filming *Fiddler on the Roof* in Europe.

Q: "And Gary Blye?"

A: "Glue."

Q: "Glue?"

A: "Glue."

Gary, 27, brother of producer Allan Blye, is associate producer and in charge of the budget, which may explain "glue." Big, dark and quiet like his brother, he was born and raised in Winnipeg and had lived in Los Angeles for 10 years. His background included a stint as assistant to Colonel Tom Parker, Elvis Presley's manager, and some years with one of the major Hollywood talent agencies.

Gary told me they had brought in $200,000 worth of sets, props, costumes, etc., for just that one show. I learned that one episode costs about $150,000 to produce and one minute of advertising time runs to around $70,000. Gary said it takes 225 people to put the show together and that studio time costs $3,000 an hour. I wanted to know what people were paid but Gary would say only that the Canadians were probably making 50 to 75 percent more than at home.

He figured that he, his brother and Chris Beard, the other producer, worked an average of 100 hours a week.

"We like what we're doing," he explained.

Q: "Billy Van, Cher?"

A: "Banana."

Q: "Banana?"

A: "Right."

A short, blond, stocky man, Billy has been described as "the most versatile talent on Canadian TV" and "one of the great sketch-comedy actors in the world." An 18-year CBC veteran, he has over 2,000 TV shows under his belt. In 1960 he formed his own group, The Billy Van Four, and is still much in demand as a choral director and for singing commercials. In 1968, as a star on *Nightcap* (a CBC Toronto show), his income was estimated at $75,000.

One of the six regular performers on *S & C* (three others are also Canadian), Billy had come here three months before. Why?

"There just isn't enough work at home," he said.

Q: "Murray Langston?"

A: "Rubber face."

Producer Allan Blye called Murray "the show's all-around crazy person." Born in Nova Scotia, Murray, 28, has a long sad face and the moustache hanging over his mouth makes it sadder. Like his colleagues in the cast he is forever "on." That week it was John Wayne talk. Some may remember Murray from *Laugh-In* on which, among other disguises, he has appeared as a fork, a tube of toothpaste and a grandfather clock.

At rehearsal with all the cast pressing tightly around Sonny, Cher and guest star William Conrad, Conrad suddenly roared, "Somebody bit my ankle!" He glared at the giggling performers and pointed, "That moustached Canadian bastard!" In a weepy voice, Murray Langston yelled back, "Get me a part on *Cannon* then!"

Q: "Peter Cullen?"

A: "Master of all trades."

Cullen, 32, is perhaps best known as a cast member of CBC network productions like *Funny You Should Say That*, *Comedy Crackers* and *Zut!* One of his characters was a French Canadian who cut off arguments with "Don't press my nerve!" Short and energetic, Cullen was once pee-wee boxing champion of Montreal, his hometown. On *S & C* he announces, does the animated voices and is a regular on camera. Blye said of him, "He has any voice in the world in his throat."

Peter said this about his work in Canada: "The CBC is run for and by bureaucrats. There are too many people in high positions whose only concern is not to lose that power. . . . There's a lack of trust and a terrible pettiness."

This about work in Los Angeles: "You make it on talent. There's more respect for an actor. And the opportunities! I'm so close to biting success, I can taste it. But I say, 'Go slow, stay cool, don't blow it—it *is* going to happen.'

"And where else but in California can you have lunch with Jonathan Winters and play tennis with Scott Carpenter the same day?"

Q: "How about Ted Zeigler?"

A: "Ace number one."

The story goes that when Zeigler came to see Chris Beard for work and mentioned that for eight years in Montreal he was Johnny Jellybean, the host of a children's show, Beard jumped up and shouted, *"Johnny Jellybean!* You're hired for the rest of your life."

Zeigler has wavy hair and looks 10 years younger than his 46. As a face puller there are few in his league. To help ease studio tedium and tension everybody, including the Bonos, works hard for laughs. Zeigler seemed consistently to top them all.

We had a short chat once that didn't start off well. Zeigler wore a bowler pulled so low it folded his ears in half.

"Hi," he said, his voice deep and oozing warmth.

There followed a moronic smile, a face like a fish, and a fierce frown.

"Well, that was very enjoyable," he said heartily, and walked away.

But he came back and I learned he was writing two screenplays, some material for *The Bobby Darin Show*, doing a variety of announcing and commercial chores, and just finishing a *Li'l Abner* special.

Zeigler has been a clown in a tea room, an Easter Bunny and a department store Santa Claus. There was a possibility, he said, he might return and do Johnny Jellybean again this summer. I had the impression that entertaining children was still his first love.

Q: "And Jimmy Dale?"

A: "Mr. Easy-does-it."

The show's 37-year-old musical director came from England to Canada when he was 12. He went to work in Los Angeles four years ago and brought his family along. Recently he had moved back to Toronto—"Better for the kids"—and now commuted.

I didn't see much of him as he was always holed up somewhere writing music. At least once that week he was at it 24 hours nonstop.

But he did tell me that the problem with the CBC was "lack of money and you're stuck with bad personnel and facilities, and you can't go shopping for better"; and the problem with Hollywood was that "you get typed too easy."

During a rehearsal early in the week Dale, seated at the piano, said gently to Cher, seated in a canvas director's chair, "You just sing it the way you want to." Cher looked up at him from her music and with a long fingernail hooked away some hair from her face. Then she said very distinctly, "That is what I usually do."

Q: "Bob Arnott and Paul Wayne?"

A: "Freaked out."

There are nine writers, four of them, including Blye and Beard, from Canada. They work in teams so that they can bounce ideas off each other. I was told writers are paid between $1,000 and $1,500 per episode, or per week.

Before coming West three years ago, Bob Arnott had 10 years with the CBC. He wrote for, among others, Wayne and Shuster and Tommy Hunter, and produced Max Ferguson's show for a while.

A soft-spoken man in his late 30s, he said he missed Canada a lot.

"People are weird here," he confided. "Nobody *walks*."

"One thing about us: There isn't a Canadian I know who's taken out citizenship papers."

Paul Wayne, 40, born and raised in Toronto, had eight years with the CBC and many TV plays to his credit when he arrived in Hollywood in 1964. Shows he has done, aside from *S & C*, include *The Carol Burnett Show*, *Bewitched*, *All in the Family* and *The Smothers Brothers Comedy Hour*.

Wayne had a succinct way of speaking.

"Had to write a show in London two years ago," he said. "Stopped off in Toronto and phoned old friends—everybody, but everybody, had moved to Los Angeles. A giant transplant. Maybe it's a jungle here, but at least there's work."

I asked if the relationship with the two producer-writers wasn't sometimes difficult, even ego-bruising, for the other seven word-men.

"No," said Wayne. "Blye and Beard don't come on as the kings of comedy. No sarcasm, no putdowns, nothing to inhibit you. There is respect. Eccentric ideas are welcomed. And I guess their willingness to try things creates a desire to do the best you can."

Wayne had probably pinpointed one of the reasons for the phenomenal success of Blye and Beard in Hollywood. A few of the other shows they've written or produced, or both, include *The Smothers Brothers Comedy Hour*, *Laugh-In*, and the Glen Campbell and Andy Williams productions. Coming up are at least two summer series and deals are brewing on a slew of specials.

Q: "Chris Beard, Cher?"

A: "Maniac."

"This is a political town," Beard told me. "Allan and I have never won an award because we're from Canada. Eight nominations for *Sonny and Cher* but it was Art Fisher who got it. We're smart-assed Canadians who've taken away a lot of work. We won't win anything this year either!"

An explosive man, Beard, 36, has red and blonde hair sprouting out from all over his head and looks like a mad Viking. He was born in England, moved to Australia as a teenager and came to Canada in the early 60s. For four years he wrote, produced and performed CBC Toronto's funny and daring *Nightcap*.

When I was there he did audience warmups (only about a quarter of *S & C* is taped before an audience) and, for a Dickensian carol-singing sketch, he donned cape and hat and joined the cast.

Beard was hired as a writer on *Laugh-In* in 1968.

"I thought I had it made then," he said.

We were sitting in the empty stands watching Sonny and Cher rehearse a song intro with their daughter Chastity.

"But after about six months," Beard went on, "it dawned on me that I knew so much more than the people out here and so . . . !"

Under the lights, Sonny and Cher were coaxing Chastity to say, "Ho-ho-ho, Merry Christmas everybody!" But Chastity wouldn't. Cher told her softly,

"Don't be an ass, say it!" Sonny promised, "After you say it you can go and play." So then she did. But there was more to the intro than that, and Chastity couldn't go and play.

"This show is a great deception," said Beard.

"Sonny really can't sing much or dance. Cher, of course, is terrific. But the reason it works is that we show just that. Those two have magic though. . . . What we do is give them tremendous glamour and then satirize that glamour, satirize Hollywood."

How come there are so many Canadians on the show?

"Because they're our friends," said Beard. "We know what they can do."

Q: "And Allan Blye?"

A: "Papa."

According to director Art Fisher, Blye is "the best TV comedy-variety editor on the planet." And editing is important on this show.

Though unobtrusive, Allan projects his authority unmistakably.

"In TV," he said, "we're past the time of 'an eye on the stage.' The tube is unique and we're trying to use it for what it is. And the viewers love it. They're writing asking how the technicalities are done. Nowadays they're very expert—and don't forget it!

"The key word for what we're doing—and it's nothing heavy, just entertainment—is taste. Taste and style and flow."

In 1953 in Winnipeg, Blye won an amateur singing contest which led to a regular radio spot. Since then he had acted and sung in countless Canadian radio and TV shows (500 in one three-year stretch), written numerous TV specials, a syndicated children's program, and so on.

"When I came to LA," he recalled, "people asked, 'Why work so hard, you banana?' But they're the same hours as in Canada, and there I was a full-time cantor, too.

"The point is they're desperate for good people here. Really, really desperate. . . .

"For me it's all a dream come true. Hobbies have become a career. I believe you must have fun in what you do—or don't do it."

And so, after everybody else has done their bit on *S & C*, Blye has his fun. For 50 to 60 hours he will ply his special skills. A show of 2,000 shots may take 220 editings. In all manner of tricky ways, he'll cut, shuffle and pace the material, crafting it into the easy, flowing, believable production millions finally see.

Q: "So they're all really groovy, eh, Cher?"
A: "Love 'em."

13. My Aquarium Is Not So Much a Place for Fish as for People (1973)

First there was the crow. Shortly after dawn, just above us in the trees, it suddenly began a terrific cawing session. Tent-mate Chris Brown slept on. Eventually, the bird took off and peace returned—and lasted for what seemed three seconds. A voice started to prattle out front. A man's voice, brutally cheerful, that wouldn't stop. Chris sat upright, one eye open, the other shut and swollen from a mosquito bite. Like inside all tents in the morning it was stuffy. I crawled deeper into my sleeping bag but the voice didn't go away. I recognized its slightly high pitch. It rattled on about it being late, about already having had breakfast, about the tide being precisely right, about rising and shining. . . .

"And our chronicler then?" it wanted to know. "Is our Boswell awake? Have you brought boots? It's the most exquisite beach with outcroppings of rock to hop along. . . . Well, I've got a second pair—lucky you! Size nine. What's yours?"

I didn't answer.

"Well?"

"Eight and a half!" I shouted.

The voice sounded pleased with the shout. "Wear extra socks," it said, and went away.

So the first three thoughts that morning were: that it was great to be camping on Vancouver Island's west coast on a specimen-collecting trip for the Vancouver Public Aquarium; that it was wonderful to be woken thus by the aquarium's director, Murray Arthur Newman; that I would much rather be home in my own bed.

The one-eyed Chris didn't stop to think. It was a Saturday last June and the tide at Long Beach was about at its lowest point. Perfect for catching sea creatures, but it wouldn't stay low long. The aquarium has held the expeditions for the past seven years. Some of their families and a half-dozen keen amateurs come too. It is an outing.

Another reason Chris hurried is that he's Newman's executive assistant. Newman has a way of spurring his staff. He has this effect on a lot of people. And that's been good for Vancouver and the rest of the country. Since he was hired in 1955 to run the city's new aquarium, he has created the largest and finest institution of its kind in Canada and one of the three best on the continent. Three-quarters of the earth is covered with water and an exciting display of what lives there is a viable contribution. Vancouver made him Man of the

Year in 1964; Ottawa gave him the Centennial Medal in 1967.

And finally, to Chris, that easy patter had been the boss speaking. And Newman is very much the boss. "He's up *there*," a senior staffer told me. "He never stifles anyone, but occasionally he will browbeat." And at the aquarium, incidentally, Newman is also a kind of "star". Most accomplishments, whether his or not, usually are credited to him. Only one living thing outshines him, the beautiful Skana, 6,500 pounds and 20 feet of killer whale. You have to smile when you look at Skana, which isn't necessarily so with Newman.

Fog still clung to the rocks and water when we drove onto the beach. The retreating Pacific had bared one of the richest marine fauna areas along B.C.'s coast. Most of the specimen hunters were there, including the director and his wife Kathy. They were like children at an Easter egg party. They ran back and forth with their findings, showing them off, calling the Latin names. Each creature was deposited in a special container for shipment to the aquarium. They caught sea anemones, sunflower starfish, all sorts of rockfishes, sculpins, lingcod, and Lord knows what. Gil Hewlett, the 31-year-old curator, said he was pleased.

When I met Newman, he said, "What do you want—words or pics?" No more chatter.

"We'll take a stroll," he said.

But that didn't pan out because someone in a diving suit had spotted a huge octopus. The man had to squirt a little bleach on it to get it to come out of the rocks. Newman in hip boots splashed over with his camera. He filmed everything in sight those two days on the island. Much of what he shoots is used in lectures. It has also found a place in the 13 half-hour documentaries he made with CBC Vancouver last year, the six he'll do this year, and the network series he hopes for in 1975.

It was several hours before Newman untangled himself from the scene on the beach. We drove inland a way.

He didn't look what he was: a dreamer of large dreams; a scuba diver; a world traveler; a keen sailor; an executive running a $5 million plant; an audacious promoter; and a teacher. The round, pale face didn't show much of any of it; the body didn't look hardy. The blue eyes were very clear but didn't convey much either. Strictly a desk-bound academic—but the man's energy belied that. It seemed rationed carefully but when it was expended it came in great rushes. Ideas, wit and action poured forth and he wasn't excessively patient then. There was also the impression Newman should have been an Englishman. Born in Chicago, he had always lived in North America. (He's a Canadian citizen now.) But there was a cool sureness, a remoteness, a firm notion of privacy that were purely British.

In the car he talked easily about the aquarium and his job, hardly at all about himself. (The closest was in commenting once on the distance maintained from his staff. "Who can know, really know others?" he asked. "How do you *know* them? How do they get to *know* me?")

"We've got ambition," he said. "We want to build the greatest aquarium in the world. With display, educational and research facilities, we want to make Canadians more aware of our animals and their environment. Ironically, my aquarium is not so much a place for fish as for people.

"We all mouth 'ecology,' but what *is* the relationship of animals to their habitat? They know in the universities, but the general public, no. That's the job of aquariums and zoos—to inform, to speak for the animals. Make it interesting, scintillating and also profound. . . . Ideally, we ought to be like great temples, like railway stations."

Newman wasn't shy about the run of his career.

"I'm very widely recognized in my field," he said. "I could probably have any job I wanted if it were open.

"I'm also probably the only director who has managed an aquarium's entire development. It's an incredibly creative job. . . . It's my aquarium."

The land and building of "my aquarium" are owned by the City of Vancouver. It is maintained, though, by a non-profit society, with a budget of $800,000. Housed in a meticulously clean, graceful, one-story building, the displays have a flow and unity of design that compel attention. There's also a research wing with four laboratories and the education program involves 20,000 students.

The aquarium now has 8,600 specimens, representing 650 species of B.C. and tropical marine and fresh-water animals, on display. The basement is a plumber's nightmare: with 10 miles of piping, 3,000 gallons of water are pumped through 12 filtration systems. It costs $17,000 a year just to feed the mammals. Among other things, they eat 60.5 tons of herring yearly.

"It's a success," said Newman, "because it's a participatory institution. Housewives, industrialists, handicapped children and retired generals are active. Talented people usually have an interest in animals, and people with ability, and people with power.

"My job," said Newman, "is getting the ideas and promoting them—biological promotion. That's what I'm best at, I guess. I don't really tell people what to do. I make it possible for them to do it."

The remainder of the weekend he was always at the centre of things and there weren't many chances to talk to him. Later during a few visits in Vancouver, he always returned to the same themes:

"The world is being homogenized. The diversity of animals is rapidly disappearing. . . . Aquariums and zoos should be producers, not only consumers of animals. We should be cultural institutions, not merely places of entertainment. We should engage the highest calibre staff. We should be above and beyond the petty priorities of city governments.

"To have empathy with animals you must live with them. Some say it's wrong to keep them in captivity. But it's important for people to see. People here now know the hundreds of creatures in our harbour. The government at one point seriously thought of reducing killer whales. In 1964 we acquired the first killer whale in captivity. People's attitude changed. Legislation was put in to protect killer whales, instead. That was caused by public awareness."

In his home one night, with Vivaldi in the background, Newman talked about dreaming.

"I'm a loner, I guess. I'm a dreamer. Being remote from people allows me to dream up the things I dream.

"I would like to display more of the world's aquatic life, especially the Arctic. It would be interesting to show the interconnection of human ecology, of the Eskimos, say, and aquatic ecology. It might be possible some time to develop an aquatic garden surrounding the aquarium. I'd like to build an aquatic bird centre, enlarge the penguin display. . . . As a hobby I'm now working on the idea of a mirror-image of the aquarium in or near Vancouver for terrestrial animals."

And then he mentioned two dreams he's particularly warm about. A lot of Newman's dreams, of course, are realized.

"This involvement with great sea creatures is thrilling," he told me. "Once we brought home six narwhals from the Arctic. They all died. That was my biggest failure. But we know something about them now. I want to go back and catch more.

"And there's the coelacanth!"

The coelacanth is the rarest fish.

A preserved specimen, weighing 170 pounds and five feet long, is on display in the aquarium. Mean-looking with big teeth, only 70 have been caught to date. Until 1938 scientists thought them extinct for 60 million years. They are found in the Comore Islands off the east coast of Africa. Extraordinarily inaccessible, they may live at depths not reached by hand-lines. Newman's dream is to be the first to catch and exhibit one—live!

"It would turn the world upside down!" he said.

He is planning an expedition next January. "We've only got three problems," he told me. "Political, financial and technical."

The Comores are owned by France which may not be keen on such a scoop for Canada; it's obviously an extremely expensive venture; once caught, the mysterious coelacanth will likely prove very hard to keep alive and to transport.

Newman has already dispatched a young biologist to investigate the difficulties. I was in his office during one of their discussions. The enthusiasm was infectious. Newman fired a string of instructions and ended with:

"I'm not interested in theory. I'm interested in substance. . . . There may be an M.A. in this for you!"

Then he dialled a friend in Ottawa.

He explained his political problem and asked for advice. He listened for a moment and interrupted: "Hey! It's a French place, right? We've got a French PM. We've got a French PM who scuba dives. Can't you get him to go there when we do? That would fix it!"

Murray Newman the promoter. An outrageous idea, but one that could conceivably work. I don't know what the friend replied.

But to go back to the little expedition on Vancouver Island. On the second day a class of high school students came to help the biologists seine for specimens. They worked hard with the men dragging the net to shore and sifting its contents. Newman ran about filming. But after a while he put the camera away. He started slowly to walk along the beach. He wasn't alone long before a dozen youngsters joined him. He pointed to the thousand bits of life on the wet sand that most of us never notice. He talked about algae and fish and blennies. He made witty remarks and encouraged questions.

"There's so much to learn," he told them, again and again.

He moved a boulder and showed the incredible variety of things that lived under it. Then he carefully let the stone settle back.

"A good conservationist," said Newman, "when he lifts a rock to look underneath always returns it to its original position."

The little group moved on without haste. The tide was coming in.

14. "Bitaemo" to the Town of Dauphin, Manitoba (1975)

Printed on flags, flyers and posters, the word was out and all over town. And people kept saying the word. For four days last August, in a small community 220 miles northwest of Winnipeg, some 50,000 people kept saying it. The word had called them from across Canada, the U.S., and even South America. And as they poured into Dauphin they saw it first on the wide banner that spanned Main Street—*Bitaemo!* It's pronounced vee-tie-amo and means "welcome" in English. But once a year, English is not the tongue of Dauphin. It is Ukrainian.

And it was Ukrainians who thronged the streets. Ukrainians small and Ukrainians large, come to dance and sing Ukrainian, to take in Ukrainian art and food, to have one whale of a good Ukrainian time. Outside the Ukraine itself, there's only one place you can do that—at Canada's National Ukrainian Festival.

Thus the hordes descended on Dauphin (pop. 8,900). They turned it into a "little Ukraine." They packed motels, private homes and camping grounds, they had their noses burnt by the prairie sun, and they didn't quit dancing until 3 a.m. It's happened eight years in a row.

With a budget this year of $100,000, the festival was organized by some 100 volunteers and one paid secretary. The first one was held in 1966 in an effort to bring more tourists to Dauphin. Each year, apparently, the event grows bigger and better. In 1970, for instance, there were 17 entries for the amateur talent competition, last August 190. A sense of permanency is developing.

The emphasis was on the cultural heritage from the old country—songs, dances, music, painting, embroidery, and so on; and on the lifestyle of the Ukrainian settlers who started coming here 75 years ago, those tough and tenacious men and women who did so much to open the West.

So while the mood had a little of a country fair—there was also an old woman who read cards with terrible accuracy—it had much more of Expo 67. This even showed on Main Street; Ukrainian music came ceaselessly from loudspeakers, but softly; decorations like flags and paper flowers came in pastel shades and were easy on the eye.

Many visitors wore embroidered white shirts or blouses, or suspenders and baggy pants, or printed dresses and wide hats, or faded jeans and no shoes, or smart city suits, or T-shirts that said, "Kiss me, I'm Ukrainian." There were lined and leathery faces, red and round faces, but very few pale faces. I saw men with arms so muscled they stood away from their sides, and girls that came out of fairy tales.

They all had a lot to do in those four days. A single day could go like this: They might wander from the curling rink, which held art and artifact exhibits, to the hockey rink where the talent contestants did regular shows. Then a stop at the open-air bake ovens where a family of farmers made bread all day. Next, perhaps, onto Main Street for the parade, or polka dancing, or to buy a peach. Back again to the curling rink to see flail threshing by powerful men in their 70s, a woman artist painting *pysankas* (Easter eggs), the wooden farm tools the old people used. And they might get a *"Bitaemo!"* from a man in a straw hat in a booth full of books and papers and learn there are 583,000 Ukrainians in Canada and 20 Ukrainian weekly newspapers.

Not counting the late-night dancing and sundry parties, the Grandstand Show in the ball park would probably be the day's last stop. Since it was the festival's highlight, it was wise to eat first—the show could last from two hours to four. So maybe some *borsch,* boiled *pirohy,* rice-bacon-cabbage rolls, and baked garlic sausage on rye.

Always present at the grandstand were the *hospodar* and *hospodynia,* the festival's host and hostess, this year Joseph and Mary Lesawyer from Jersey City, New Jersey. As was repeatedly said at the opening ceremony, the event was rather *international.*

The show's producer and emcee was big and hearty Cecil Semchyshyn. A consultant in Manitoba's department of tourism, recreation and cultural affairs, he was also a singer, actor and director. Three times he was moved to tears, as was nearly everybody else, by the haunting songs of William Howika and grandson Ivan Pitkowich. The two accompanied themselves on *leeras,* ancient instruments blind beggars used to play.

"There's a resurgence of the culture our fathers brought," Cecil told me once. "It's happening with other ethnic groups, too. This diversity is healthy. We're developing an identity.... It's slightly tongue-in-cheek—but still for real, sincere."

Spectators usually numbered around 7,000. Their pride in the performers, most of them pros, was almost tangible. If rhythmic clapping was needed, 14,000 hands went at it. Presumably, it was a singular audience: it knew and understood the dances and songs. Mary Bochenko, 23, and sister Irene, 17, had sat in a bus for 21 hours from Lethbridge. It was their first visit. They were up front at every show. "Fantastic!" the girls whispered. "Fantastic!"

The singers, particularly, often seemed to evoke a longing for the old country, a land most of the crowd had never seen and never would. But someone like Mary could say, "Gosh, I'd like to go over some day! Live there!" And maybe she would.

The dance groups were the most exciting. The blazing costumes, the red soft-leather boots, the wild leaping and heel-kicking of the men, the intricate swaying and floating of the girls. . . .

The Ukrainian visitors, no doubt, went home filled with the festival's colour and spirit. To a non-Ukrainian some of it was foreign and couldn't all be grasped in a few days. It was a pleasure trying, though. And next year, in Dauphin, the *Bitaemo!* signs will be out again.

15. Learning the Ropes (1973)

Clutching his stomach, Gordie Moore lay face-down in the dried mud. It had been a brief, fierce struggle. Running like crazy, the free calf had already reached the pen at the far end of the corral. Some 20 cows stood bawling there for calves still in the chute. Their bawling filled the summer air and never let up. Gordie curled himself into a ball and rocked back and forth with his eyes shut tight. Boys and grown men moved around him, some on horseback, all twirling noose-ended ropes. Gordie's father, Gary, and his brother, Dan, were among them. So was teacher Kenny McLean. His mother, Hazel, sat on the tiny spectator stand chatting with a neighbour. Long-haired girls in faded jeans watched from atop the corral fence.

Gordie rocked another half minute. Then he slowly got to his feet, stumbled to the fence, and sat down with his head between his knees. Someone threw his hat after him.

"What's wrong with Gordie, Hazel?" I asked.

Hazel Moore is a warm and attractive rancher's wife. She likes to laugh, sit around flaming logs and sing, and have lots of folks visiting. She and Gary have three children, but there are always half a dozen more around.

Hazel glanced at her hunched-over 12-year-old.

"Whatever it is, it'll make him tougher," she said, and went on talking.

That's ropin' school for you. Either get in there and learn to handle the powerful little calves, and maybe get walloped in the belly—or stay home and watch TV. Nobody cares whether you're 12 or four times 12. It's cattle, horses, sweat, and men in there. And maybe rope burns, twisted ankles, pulled muscles, bloody noses, and broken fingers. Getting hurt is easy. No calf wants to get roped, heaved on its back and trussed up. They don't like it and they won't co-operate. To do it right and fast takes skill, practice and nerve. You learn how in roping school.

Gordie took a couple of deep breaths and wobbled back to class.

Roping schools are common in the West. It's useful to be good with a rope in cattle country—though it's less important than in the old days—and it can be very profitable at rodeos. Rodeo is a big business that is spreading. There will be more than 60 out West this year and 18 are scheduled in Ontario. In the U.S., attendance records and gate receipts reportedly show it has climbed to second place in sports after baseball.

You need only 12 enthusiasts to get a school going. One instructor can't properly handle more than that. Each student brings his own horse, rope (about 25 feet) and "piggin string" (six feet). Then you find a pro and pay him a large enough fee so he'll quit the circuit for a week.

Gary Moore, a well-to-do rancher from Dawson Creek, B.C., 380 miles northwest of Edmonton, was able to recruit his friend Kenny McLean for his school. McLean, 34, from Vernon, B.C., is one of the top all-around rodeo riders in the world.

Each of the students paid $175 for five days tuition. McLean worked them from 10 to 12 hours a day. They ranged in age from Gordie to a man near 50. School was held mostly at the Moore place, and when it rained, in an arena in town. Women prepared and delivered food to wherever school was held. Gigantic quantities of it were piled on long tables and friends and relations who had come to watch were expected to dig in as well.

But meals never lasted long. While the ranchers and ranchers' sons had taken the week off from work, and thus it was a sort of holiday, they were intent upon improving their roping. And so was McLean.

While he's friendly enough, he isn't an excessive talker. He's better at doing. And so, quietly, relentlessly, he kept his students working. Twirling the ropes till they whistled, the pupils lassoed bales of hay, hour after hour. McLean wandered among the deadly serious dozen, commenting tersely:

"Don't watch the rope, Pete—watch the bale!"

"Tighter, Tom!"

"Straight, Dave!"

Sometimes he'd stop all action and growl:

"If you guys slowed down and did things *right,* you'd be a lot better off!"

McLean wasn't talking to beginners. All had, at one time or another, entered official competitions—even Gordie. One man looked almost as good a rider and roper as McLean himself. But on the final night they held a tryout with entry fees and small money prizes. That extra bit of reality and tension proved too much for that cowboy's nerves.

The gangly Dan Moore, 15, looked very competent, too. He plans a fulltime career in rodeo. Last year he even rode Brahman bulls. He hoped to join McLean for a month this summer working rodeos up and down Alberta.

After roping bales long enough, McLean had the students whipping piggin string around a calf's feet. McLean held the rope with the calf fighting at the end. The string between his teeth, a student would first wrestle the calf on its back—that's where Gordie got it—then loop the string once around a front leg, then two loops and a half-hitch around that leg and the two hind ones. The roper throws his arms wide then and at a rodeo the time-watch stops. The pros work this bit terribly fast. Try it sometime with a wild calf, legs all pumping in different directions.

Then McLean had the students perform the complete operation: going after the calf on horseback. McLean said the actual roping of the calf then was the single most difficult move. But no matter how expert the roper, if his horse doesn't have the speed, training and temper, he's guaranteed to lose out. The two must move as one, until the calf is roped. Then the rider leaps off and runs along the rope, which is tied to the saddle horn, to throw and tie the calf. That takes all his attention. The horse is on its own and must hold the rope just so taut. Too much slack, or a fast jerk, and the job is botched.

To warm things up, McLean would bring down a few animals himself. An unlit cigarette in his mouth, he made it look like no effort at all. But he's been at it since his teens. Even now, when he can, he gets in a half-hour bale-roping and a half-hour calf-tying a day.

I asked McLean if he could give the 10 basic rules of roping. Perhaps not every person reading this will want or need to rope anything ever, but you never know. Anyhow, McLean said he didn't have 10 rules. He said:

"Throw it straight and hard like a rock.

"Don't be in too much of a hurry.

"Practise!"

On the last night he held "exams". The students competed against one another for the small prizes. I missed that, but McLean said he felt "real good" about their efforts. Gordie Moore came first in the junior category and won $15, and said *he* felt "real good."

I didn't miss the marvellous barbecue that followed exams. The grill holding the steaks was as big as an office desk; the punch tasted like lemonade but was not lemonade. Around the huge fire sat comfortable women and lean men in big hats and spurred boots. Two played guitar and they sang songs like "Red River Valley" and "Home on the Range." It only started getting dark around 11 but the singing went on and on. In the distance cattle complained, children fell asleep in their mothers' arms, occasionally a horse snorted.

16. Reporting a War's Aftermath (1973)

SINAI PENINSULA, KILOMETRE 101—The car sped northeast through the dark and every mile toward Tel Aviv was one further away from the obscenity that lay behind. Up front, the driver and our Israeli military escort talked quietly in Hebrew; in back with me, the other reporter, a stylish Englishman, lay curled asleep. The car's sloping rear window gave full view of the night sky. Minutes earlier, the sun had left a blood-red warning before ducking behind the waves of sand. Briefly the sky had glowed red, then orange, then purple, which swiftly turned to blue-black as stars winked on the furthest reaches. The land chilled instantly. I had witnessed that same sudden sunset the week before—but then I had been moving west, again away from the same obscenity, this time to Cairo, Egypt.

That's the only word for a battlefield, obscenity—young men killing and maiming one another. And after the thunder has stilled and the black smoke lifted, and the dead and wounded are carted away, then what is left behind is obscene, too. Lining the road and dotting the hills are the burned-out wrecks of tanks, trucks, armored troop-carriers, jeeps, and ambulances. Inside many of them, men had fried to death. These warped hulks are too large for desert wind to quickly bury in the sand. Encircling each vehicle is pathetic debris that testifies men were really there—bits of scorched clothing, cans of food, a tennis shoe, a spilt package of salt pills, and, always, at least one shaving brush. I was in Egypt and Israel for about three weeks late this year after the cease-fire. On the fronts of both countries and on the Israeli side of the Golan Heights, I spotted at least three dozen shaving brushes, their bristles worn with use.

"Tension in the Middle East" is a phrase that has lost all meaning. It's simply been a fact for 25 years. We've grown immune to bad news from there. Since Israel became a state in 1948, the tension has flared into full-scale war four times, and yes, then we did pay attention—because it might involve us. This last war certainly did. Over the years, hundreds of plans have been devised to bring "just and lasting peace," and, at the United Nations, millions of words have been argued. Russia and America—but not only they—have fed the warring factions billions of dollars' worth of weaponry and military know-how and simultaneously pressed and bullied them to come to terms—and are doing so now. Yet, at this writing, Arabs and Israelis are dug into the sands of the Sinai and the hills of the Golan Heights facing Syria, ready to start the slaughter again.

We had set out from Tel Aviv at 3:00 a.m.; the journey to and from the Suez front would take 18 hours. I was flying home the next day and wasn't sorry this was to be my last frontline trip. In fact, I didn't much regret leaving the Middle East. The air in Egypt and Israel, and presumably in Syria where I wasn't allowed in, seems to be charged with two terrible contradictions. On the one hand, there are thousands of young men, backed by immense arsenals, poised to kill or be killed; on the other hand, those same men and all their relations at home are hoping and praying for peace. No one wants war. Everyone wants peace. But fear and hatred rule in these lands, and most believe that peace will not come for a very long time.

What struck me was the unreality, or surreality, of much that I saw. Take the visits to the fronts: equipped with hotel-prepared lunch boxes, journalists set out in air-conditioned buses or comfortable taxis. They drove for hours in the company of fellow reporters, generally as ill-informed as they were themselves. Then there were hurried stops at places that showed much war havoc, bombed towns, or the remains of especially ferocious field battles. Under the watchful eye of military or government escorts, they were allowed a few pictures and perhaps a brief word with a soldier. Back into the bus or car then and on to the next pre-picked spot, much as they might have toured the pyramids or Jerusalem's holy places.

The first such trip I made was with 120 other press people in two buses. We drove from Cairo to Port Said at the Mediterranean entrance of the Suez Canal. Once 100 ships a day passed through Port Said's harbour but, like the canal, it now hadn't functioned in six years. It had been heavily bombed in 1967 and again this past October. Most of its population had been relocated. As we neared the city, military traffic increased; bulldozers heaved earth aside to make hiding holes for men, guns, and tanks. Soldiers waved triumphant fists or fingered victory signs. We reporters were tourists.

In one of the few still intact rooms of Port Said's city hall, the city's governor, a retired major general, gave a press conference. Through a translator, he talked for a long time about the bravery and suffering of his people. In the middle of the room, a light bulb dropped from its socket in the ceiling and burst on the floor with a considerable bang.

The governor, perhaps accustomed to artillery, didn't react. He sat at a table, shouted much of what he had to say, and, beneath the table, his booted feet danced nervously. The reporters grew bored. None of it was hard news. The governor finally said Port Said was proud to receive us and were there any questions. Yes, two: What was the city's population before 1967 and what was it now? The governor said it used to be 300,000 and now was 50,000. The press conference had taken one hour.

In front of city hall, Egyptian soldiers obligingly posed on a captured Israeli tank until an officer told them to stop it. Of the 50,000 civilians, we saw perhaps ten. The city was empty. We were driven through long, wide streets, swept clean but with ripped and torn buildings and mountains of rubble on either side. Many side streets were shut off with barbed wire. The buses dropped us off at a bombed hospital, a bombed nursery, and a bombed school. At each we had a few minutes to take pictures; TV commentators talked on camera and gesticulated at the ruination around them.

When we were hustled aboard again after the school, there were grumbles of "Goddamn propaganda."

An Egyptian TV reporter whose sound- and camera-men hadn't turned up said that, if his crew had been there, he could have done some "marvelous sob stuff." He intoned, "What you see were once homes where people lived, loved, laughed, cried and died. Now they are ruins furnished with nothing but sorrow."

We crossed by ferry to the harbour's east side and the town of Port Fuad. More silent streets of destroyed homes, toppled telephone poles, mangled trees. We stopped at a mosque with half its roof blown off. Speaking through an interpreter, an officer told us that 200 civilians had been killed in the two communities and 600 wounded. He said that in the October War Israelis had made 357 sorties. He was looking at the mosque while talking and, from the tone of his voice, he could have been telling us the building's age and various measurements.

Back into the bus and off to the desert. Past fenced-off minefields and dugouts pointing the wrong way—Israel had occupied this area a few weeks earlier. Then came the first of the burned-out tanks and trucks and jeeps, of which I was to see hundreds. We were heading for one of the Bar-Lev Line's "strong points," which the Egyptians had overrun in the first days of the war and promptly dynamited. The self-contained combat units were now a mess of concrete, wire, split sand bags, and shredded tires.

Some Egyptian soldiers were coaxed to face east with stern faces and raised guns. Later I would see Israelis do the same thing looking west. Photographers scurried about for angles, risking entanglement with huge banks of barbed wire. TV crews maneuvered commentators in front of "war-like" backdrops. Stone-faced, the escorts watched us at play.

And under the sun, which had grown hot and yellow, some of us were also watching one of us. He had thick, black, wavy hair, and a magnificent smile, and he wore a beige suit, white turtleneck sweater and soft, calf-leather boots. He looked like a film star.

He was Japanese and spoke no English, nor did the others on his TV crew.

At every stop, they were the first out of the bus, and Beige Suit would instantly start commentating. He would talk steadily, the camera following his every gesture, until ordered back aboard.

All together, they must have recorded at least an hour's commentary.

But later that day, the team did catch a remarkable bit of film. On our way back to Cairo, we had stopped on the outskirts of Port Said for gas. It was just another empty, bombed street. Some of the journalists sat dozing. But the Japanese were out like a flash, and once again the star was chatting, pointing, and showing teeth. A few of us got out to watch him close-up. We stood behind the camera-man and then somebody giggled and our self-control was gone. A dozen grown men stood in that demolished street and laughed until tears started coming. The star looked at us, smiled, and, next thing, the camera was recording the world press with open mouths and shaking bodies against that sad background.

The second bus was being tanked. Back in my own, I stared drowsily out the window. At the far end of the lifeless street a car was slowly approaching. It was a white Mercedes, its headlights painted blue. As it got closer, I saw the driver was a very straight-backed military man wearing his cap. As the car moved beneath my window, one of my hands pinched the other: sitting up on the back seat, looking left and right, was a big black poodle.

Some days later, the Egyptian press office organized another trip. It was to Kilometre 101, the tiny clutch of tents on the Cairo-Suez road, where the Egyptian and Israeli generals met to negotiate disengagement of forces, a truce. This time, 114 press people made the journey.

The main tent, roped off and ringed by blue-helmeted UN emergency forces, bayonets fixed to their rifles, flew the UN flag. On the Israeli side, the white star on blue had been raised over a machine-gun nest. The Egyptians showed no flag, but they had set up a big tent for the press, and served lemonade and cookies.

The generals arrived and disappeared into the tent before anyone had time to focus. Time passed slowly. An increasingly stronger wind blew down the Israeli flag. Soldiers bunched together and pushed to straighten the pole. About seventy cameras trained on that bit of excitement. But then the wind really started whipping and, in minutes, we were in a sandstorm. We hid in the buses and in the hospitality tent.

In the tent, the *Newsweek* correspondent was holding court. Dressed in starched khaki, his own name stenciled over one shirt pocket, *Newsweek* over the other, he was giving interviews. The week before, when no other newsman in Cairo had been allowed to go to Kilometre 101, that small, immaculately groomed man had lodged at the checkpoint in an Egyptian bunker. He called the Egyptian officers by their first names, and knew more about what was happening than anyone else. There had been a press conference where a hundred foreign journalists had come in from Israel, and he had been the only one from the other side. His colleagues didn't love him for it.

I had heard that this was the twelfth war that he had reported. When, later, I asked him a few questions, that was the first thing he told me. Then he described some shooting incidents, or "teasing," across the cease-fire line. The blue eyes shone as he described precisely how, where, and at what time two Egyptians had been killed the night before.

The flies, also hiding in the tent from the wind, were getting annoying, when there was a shout from outside: "General al-Gamasy is coming!"

Clearly in a hurry, the tall Egyptian had gotten only as far as the rope when the swarm of reporters was upon him. An officer hastened to his aid and yelled into the blowing sand, "The general has nothing to say!" The general had to go to the toilet.

Twenty minutes later, another flurry of action. An over-zealous United Nations Emergency Force (UNEF) MP, a Finn, was pushing an Italian cameraman away from the rope cordoning off the negotiating tent. He was wrong to do so since the Italian was on Egyptian ground and it was up to Egyptian MPs to check his movements. From the buses and the tent the war correspondents came running, led by the American covering his twelfth war. Cameras whirred. Had the young Finn made one false move, or said a wrong word, that young Finn would have made headlines around the world. It's what's called news-making.

Three-and-a-half hours later, the generals emerged from the tent. We rushed to the rope. One sentence was all the hard news that day from Kilometre 101: "The talks were useful and will continue tomorrow."

A few days later, I was being driven in a taxi to the Golan Heights in the north of Israel. Soldiers were out on the highways hitching rides to the front after 48-hour leaves. We didn't have room because, besides the driver and myself, there was a large, middle-aged British reporter and, of course, our military escort.

As we started the climb to the Heights, the landscape quickly grew into forsaken treeless hills of hardened lava. Occasionally, we passed through deserted Arab villages of mud huts. After Quneitra, civilian traffic ceased. The asphalt road turned into dirt. Thick mist settled over the land. The driver took care, as mines could lie on either side of us. Once more, we were encountering burned-out vehicles. We were in territory the Israelis had recently captured from Syria. Our escort had been there several times and was finding his way from memory; the driver suggested we should use the car's compass as well. We got out once to look at a badly shelled farm home. It was very quiet. A slice of wall still standing showed intricate flower patterns cut into the mud.

A few miles from the village of Mazraat Beit Jinn, which faced the actual front, checkpoint guards stopped us. There had been a lot of shooting the night before and we would need special permission from the area's commander to proceed. We tracked him down and a pass was granted with the promise we wouldn't take pictures.

Mazraat, too, had suffered severe shelling. The population had fled when the Israelis came, except for two old men, one of whom had since died. Abandoned donkeys wondered about in twos and threes scrounging for food. What rooms and stables had not been smashed served as living quarters for Israeli soldiers. Bulldozers could be heard in the hills digging new fortifications.

We stopped at a partial house nestled on a cliff, which sheltered some fifteen men. They hadn't shaved for days and looked weary. One was preparing a meal of rice, canned stew, and coffee. Four checked their guns and vanished into the mist on patrol. Two sat in a small dug-out overlooking the valley below. They had dragged in chairs from the house, and at their feet was a large can full of hand-grenades.

I wandered to the back, into what had been the barn. You could tell by the droppings on the floor where various animals had lived. One square space was covered with feathers. It was very still. Suddenly, from beneath a cluster of fallen rafters, exploded a commotion of angry flapping and cackling, and then silence again. A chicken shouldn't frighten a person like that.

Out front, we were offered coffee. I drank mine with the two men in the look-out. You couldn't stand up straight inside and it was stuffy. I asked the one who spoke English best if he ever felt afraid of the Syrians—Damascus was 25 miles away. He thought about his reply.

"I'm not afraid at this moment," he said, "but sometime I am—and then I turn very cold."

When we were about to leave, a soldier told us he had just heard that he had become a father for the second time, but it was a daughter again.

"That's a sign of peace," said a friend.

"There are lots of signs of peace," said the father, "but not *peace*."

In the car going south again, the Englishman said he wanted a Syrian helmet for his 15-year-old son who was "really keen on that sort of thing. It would make him quite the hero in school."

Two days later on the road from Tel Aviv to the Suez front in a taxi, but this time driving west, we didn't have much time to appreciate the shapes and colours of the desert before we struck the dismal rubbish of war again. Our escort was a vastly informed man on things military. He seemed determined that we, yet another English reporter and I, should become so, too. Without stop, he provided details on ruined as well as operating hardware, on different types of fortifications, mines, planes, and bombs. He cited the known numbers of soldiers killed on all sides.

"That's a lot of dead young men," observed the Englishman.

The flow of data ceased for a while.

We crossed the canal, an unimpressive strip of water, skirted a portion of the Great Bitter Lake where mines were visible only yards from shore. Thirteen ships manned by skeleton crews have lain anchored there since 1967, unable to move from the lake—thirty miles from everywhere, a million miles from anywhere.

We stopped occasionally and chatted with soldiers. One originally from South Africa said, "Yes, we fought well. But no gain in territory can make up for the casualties."

Both on the war- and home-fronts, I heard almost those identical words a hundred times and more.

We cut south to visit Suez. Entrance to the city was forbidden because there had been shooting that morning, so we drove west towards Cairo to see Kilometre 101 from the Israeli side. The tour was almost done. Only the long drive back to Tel Aviv remained.

The generals had cancelled talks that day and it was quiet. UN and Israeli flags snapped in the wind; the Egyptians still hadn't raised theirs.

We ate our hotel-prepared lunches at the checkpoint. Afterwards, we pitched the empty boxes on the pyramid-shaped garbage heap already high with cartons from reporters who had been there the previous day and the day before that. The containers were mostly labeled Tel Aviv Hilton. I remembered that, seven days earlier, a few hundred yards away, I had seen just such a pile. All those boxes had been marked Nile Hilton.

17. Samurai Swordsman (1977)

It was a warm pleasant afternoon—about half-past three, Monday, May 30, 1977, in Montreal. I had arrived a week earlier; in a few days, I would leave again. In 1959, I came to live here, and for the next 17 years it was home. Important years—middle 20s to late 30s—and mostly good years. But I had been away from Montreal now for two years, one of them in Europe, and would probably not make it home again. I regretted that, and had thought so in the days preceding this nice warm one. Wherever I settled, I would never be able to call that place mine in the same way. I know this city, feel comfortable here, concerned and involved with what happens. Much of the little I know I've learned here; who I am was largely shaped here. Most importantly, I have been allowed to love and have been loved in return here, and have made a few good friends. These thoughts had been with me since I had returned. And the night before, I sat up very late with friends and talked about them. Now, a little woozy, I walked in the heart of the city down Stanley to St. Catherine St. This is one of the busiest spots in Canada. Idling, honking cars inched along bumper to bumper; shoppers crammed the sidewalks. The cloud of noise that hung between the buildings was familiar and friendly.

I was in Montreal to sell and give away furniture and personal effects I couldn't afford to ship overseas. One item that might bring a modest sum was an old samurai sword inherited from my grandfather. I liked the carvings on the bone scabbard but had never grown attached to the thing. As a journalist, I've seen something of war and crime and, frankly, I fear and abhor tools that kill. I know some have their uses sometimes; still, they are our worst inventions.

Earlier that afternoon, I had been to an auction house to get an idea of the sword's value. A woman there had advised me to see a dealer in Oriental art on Sherbrooke near McKay St. who might give a fair price. I carried the sword wrapped in a red, green, blue, yellow, and purple-striped towel. This to protect the carving work and so people on the street wouldn't recognize it for what it was and stare.

McKay is near Stanley and I had a cheque for $100 from a friend who said his bank was on Stanley and St. Catherine. I walked into the bank with, in my right hand, the cheque and identification with my picture on it; I held the sword in my left hand. Seeing the ID, the girl in the wicket surmised I didn't have an account and said I should go to the front counter. I did so and a young man behind the counter said, "Sorry, sir, wrong bank. We're the Commerce. See, the cheque is the Royal's, across the street." He was right. I hadn't paid attention. There are two banks on Stanley and St. Catherine: the Bank of Commerce on the northeast corner, the Royal Bank on the southeast.

I remember I was humming as I walked out of the Commerce. I crossed the street between the slow-moving cars and entered the Royal.

At the first wicket, a young man with curly hair and a moustache, on seeing the identification card, told me to go to the front counter. At the counter, I lay down the sword in the towel. The plump, middle-aged lady behind the counter looked at it. I had noticed several people looking at it.

"Not to worry. It's not a gun," I said.

"So," the lady smiled, "we've all got to go sometime!"

She went off a few paces to check my friend's account in a filing cabinet. My identification card was lying photo-up on the counter. She returned and asked me to the sign the back of the cheque. She compared signatures.

"Is McKay east of here or west?" I asked.

She never answered. Her eyes widened, staring over my shoulder. An open hand smashed into the back of my head with a force that sent me sprawling against the counter. Fingers gripped my neck so fiercely that, for a moment I saw black. I couldn't breathe. I felt my eyes bulging. The voices of men yelled orders. I heard people gasp, and a small squeal from a woman. Somebody kicked at my ankles. The left, the right, and I toppled forward, my face almost hitting the counter. A fist knocked my arm sideways. I tried to look behind me but the hand on my neck was like a vise.

"Spread! Spread!"

More kicking. I wasn't spreading fast enough. That hand on my neck seemed to be jamming the signals.

"Spread, goddamn you!"

My eyes found the staring ones of the lady. "Tell them I'm cashing a cheque—*please!*"

Her eyes left mine, turned to the window on St. Catherine. People there pressed up against the glass.

"I don't know . . ." she whispered.

My left arm was wrenched behind me, turning me slightly. Steel clicked around my wrist. Now I could see him. A tall police officer wearing mirror-sunglasses was holding my neck. I'm five-foot-eight and weigh 150 pounds. He held me like a rag. A second policeman, holstering his revolver, yanked my right arm to my back and steel cuffs fastened it to my left. Three other police officers straightened out of shooting crouches. One slapped his hands along my body—frisking. Another grabbed the sword.

He cursed as the towel fell away. He partially unsheathed the sword. More gasps from the people in the back, all standing. The sword is old and the loose copper tip on the scabbard's end fell to the floor.

"Careful! It's antique!"

"Shut up!"

But he did pick up the copper tip.

Then I was being half-carried, half-dragged out of the bank. Outside, traffic had come to a standstill, the sidewalks were packed, people crowded behind windows and upper storeys. All staring at me, some pointing, their faces tight, closed. The crowd made room reluctantly to let us through, me lurching between two policemen holding me under the armpits, alternately pushing and pulling me forward. Across St. Catherine, a hundred yards up Stanley where a police van was parked. The handcuffs hurt. Just in front of the van a well-dressed young man barred our way. He was sweating.

"Happy?" he screamed at me. "Are you happy now?"

He was eased aside and I was shoved into the back of the van onto a steel bench. The door was slammed shut. One of the officers, very young with a large moustache, sat down in front with his back to me. My mouth was dry. I was breathing hard. But I wasn't afraid. Watching arrests on police shows, I've sometimes wondered if I would be. I was tense though, alert, not woozy anymore. And I was aware that I was recording everything, as if, inside my head, behind my eyes, a camera was running. I spoke to the policeman's back.

"Officer, may I ask a question?"

He didn't turn. "No."

People pressed around the van, some with their noses flat against the windows, watching me, their eyes unblinking. I looked back at them, moving slowly from face to face. Their eyes studied me, taking it all in, my shoes, my clothes, my face. They looked into my eyes. So *that* is what a criminal looks like. A second policeman climbed into the van. He carried the sword and showed it to his partner. They ran their thumbs along the edge of the blade. Without turning, one of them asked my name and birthdate, then passed them on by car phone. Minutes went by. Perhaps ten. Crazy minutes. Everything was out of kilter. This *couldn't* be happening. My thoughts raced. The handcuffs hurt. I sensed an air of waiting in the faces all around me. Waiting for what? For me to make a wrong move, so the police would have to hit me, or shoot? For me to break down and cry? I looked into hundreds of pairs of eyes in those minutes. I looked—and this was part of the craziness—for some sign of forgiveness in those eyes. Forgiveness for what? I hadn't done anything. Still, that is what I looked for because, as those minutes went by, I was receiving with great force this one message: You are guilty. You are bad.

From a cruiser parked across the street, a third policeman approached the van's single open window by the driver's seat.

"We're taking you to the station," he said to me. "Maybe later you'll be released."

I breathed easier. I wondered if I could ask my guards to take off the handcuffs now. They really hurt. I would have them on no more than 20 minutes, yet the marks would still show three hours later.

The young policeman with the moustache turned around.

"You are now under arrest. Understand?"

"But that other officer just said . . ."

When he spoke again, his voice had a soft, lazy quality.

"Under arrest. Understand?"

I nodded. I decided to be very careful about what I said to these men. There was a tension about them (later in the station, too) that did not relax and seemed to beg for relief.

We set off and slowly moved through the crowd, which had not thinned. At Station 10, a few blocks away, I was hauled out of the van and marched inside. At the "check-in" counter, I was told to spread and was frisked again. The handcuffs stayed on. Then came the questions; they were shouted. Why was I in the bank? Why in the other bank first? Why the sword? Where did I get it? Address? Occupation? Did I have a record? *Sure* I didn't have a record? My pockets were emptied. The policeman doing so held up a loose peppermint, then dropped it on the floor. There were by then nine of them gathered around. A samurai sword is not an everyday weapon. Each one had to unsheathe it and run his thumb along the blade.

They ran out of questions. The handcuffs were taken off. Nobody said anything so I asked what would happen next. I was told there would be a full investigation, and, meanwhile, I was to take off my belt and wait in the cell across from the main office downstairs. The cell was a high-ceilinged, yellowish room smelling of sweat. Angry graffiti covered the walls. Now I was alone, and I ran off the movie I had been making in my mind. Several times I had to grin—it was such an absurd incident. But mostly I felt angry in a dull, helpless way. And I still feel like that. I know far worse things have happened to people in similar circumstances. I wasn't hurt, and I wasn't beaten, and soon they would have to let me go. Still, it was an ugly, degrading affair. Through the green wire-netting of the cell door I could see policeman after policeman, plainclothes and in uniform, move up and finger the samurai. The thing fascinated them. An officer with a large stomach carrying a Styrofoam cup ambled over to my cell. For a moment, I thought he was bringing me a coffee.

"Where did you get it?"

"I inherited it from my grandfather."

"Where did he get it?"

"I don't know. He always had it."

"Want to sell it, huh?"

"Yes."

"How much?"

I felt my lower jaw sag. I had just been arrested on suspicion of holding up a bank with a samurai sword. Now, beltless, from behind steel wire, I was negotiating the sale of that same weapon with one of my captors.

"Five hundred."

He shrugged and walked away.

Minutes later, another policeman came along and unlocked the door. He didn't say anything and didn't look at me. I had been in the cell about an hour. I followed him to the counter where lay the sword, the towel, and a large envelope containing my watch, money, and so on.

"See if everything's there and sign here."

Several other policemen wandered over.

"You can go," said the man who had unlocked the door.

"I hope this has taught you a lesson," said an officer with gray hair.

I looked at their faces. It was not a joke.

"What lesson?"

The older man said nothing. Behind him, sitting on the edge of a desk and looking out the window, I recognized the policeman who had grabbed me in the neck. He wore his sunglasses. He never turned around.

"Don't carry a samurai sword into a bank?"

No response.

I stuffed my things into my pockets. The policemen watched me. The last item was a ballpoint pen.

"Thank you," I said without thinking. Then: "Hey! For what?"

There was no reaction. I felt small. I rolled up the sword in the towel, picked it up—and put it down again.

"I'm going out on the street with this. Am I going to get arrested again?"

One in the group moved. He folded the towel lengthwise and wrapped it around the centre of the sword.

"Now we can see it's a sword," he explained.

I walked out.

The oriental art dealer was closed when I got there. That night I called a friend at one of the dailies who thought the incident was hilarious and promptly wrote up a few paragraphs for next morning's edition. It was retold on several Montreal radio stations, CBC radio and television news aired the story, and a Toronto columnist used it.

I called a friend and attorney, Lorne Goldman, to find out what precisely had caused my arrest, and whether I could hold anyone responsible. Apparently, the people at the Royal Bank had been as shocked as I was when the policemen stormed in. It was, Goldman determined, Brian McMahon, assistant manager at the Bank of Commerce, the bank I went in first, who had on seeing me immediately called the police. McMahon apparently did not check with the two clerks I had spoken to in his bank who could have told him I was on a legitimate errand, only in the wrong place. The management of this branch of the Bank of Commerce as well as the bank's public relations department indicated to Goldman that there was no question they intended to provide me with any sort of satisfaction. On the contrary, it was made clear that they believed the onus was on me to apologize: I had given the assistant manager "a bad time" that afternoon.

Thus ends what's called "an experience," the sort that "makes you think." About what, though? Mostly, I fear, about indifference. It shouldn't have happened but, hell, it happens all the time. . . .

Actually, it doesn't quite end there. A few days later, I went back to cash that cheque. A friend came along. That plump lady behind the counter recognized me and we chatted and laughed about what happened. Then she became serious.

"I've worked with the public a long time, you know. I see all sorts of people. I knew you weren't a criminal. You're not the type. I knew the police had made a mistake."

And then:

"But when they came running in. . . . Well, I mean, you could have stolen that sword somewhere, couldn't you?"

18. The Good Life in a Good Place (1979)

The good life. All of us want it, most of us strive for it and, while we may differ on what it is precisely, we agree that one ingredient is vital—money. Although money isn't everything, a sizable supply helps. And good amounts of it are virtually guaranteed to at least one category of Canadians—professionals. Doctors, lawyers and accountants, to name three, earn splendid incomes: Canada's self-employed doctors reported an average income of $46,661 in 1975, lawyers, $42,731 and accountants, $34,688.

The good life is theirs for the living. But where do most doctors, lawyers and accountants live this good life? In cities: 50 percent of doctors, lawyers and chartered accountants practising in Ontario, for instance, reside in Toronto; most of the remaining professionals live in such centres as Ottawa, Hamilton and Windsor. On the surface, it's easy to see why. Cities have fine restaurants, theatres and shops, and generate a special excitement. They're also crowded, noisy, dirty, competitive, unhealthy and, sometimes, dangerous. But, perhaps most important, cities are where most of us live—the patients, the clients.

Still, a few professionals have rejected city living, and opted instead to live and work in small towns.

Exeter, Ontario, is such a town. Thirty miles north of London, Ontario, Exeter has a population of 3,500, one bookstore, seven hairdressers, eight grocers, nine churches and 10 restaurants. Incorporated in 1951, it's basically a farming community: the flat rich land that surrounds it is classified as "A" ground; there are no slums; no real charity cases. About 85 percent of town dwellers own their own homes. The air is clean, the streets quiet, and at night the silence is complete.

If you're a lawyer or an accountant or a doctor, what is it like to live and work in Exeter? Why do you come? Why do you stay?

We asked one of each. The three men (women in these professions are still rare in Canadian small towns) are about the same age, have open, cheerful natures, a liking for the outdoors and sports, attractive wives and small children, large homes, and the community's respect. Young men still, they also have this in common: they seem tranquil.

"Seven years ago, when I was still articling in Toronto, a friend asked me to join his one-man operation up here," says lawyer Keith ("Kim") McLean, 33. "That first year [McLean was admitted to the bar in 1972] I made about

$19,000—and then I was made a full partner. In the city I would have spent much more time on the bottom rung. There they may say, 'We'll talk partnership in a year,' but it probably won't happen for another five." McLean says his income is now higher than the Canadian average of $42,731. Yet, he says, he often charges less than lawyers in Toronto or London. An example: drawing up a will in the city may cost from $60 to $75; McLean charges his clients $10.

One reason he has done well, he thinks, is that he joined an established firm; it would be a lot more difficult for an outsider. Another reason: client loyalty. And that is because "we can service them better. They have more access to us. In Toronto everything is by appointment, with us it's less than half."

There is also the matter of trust. "You trust your clients, your colleagues, and they trust you," says McLean. "We *know* each other. Here we socialize much more together. A young solicitor in Toronto doesn't trust *anyone*. Here we don't even certify cheques. We take each other's word."

McLean's office is on Exeter's Main Street between Fisher's Hardware and Junction Department Store. You can see him at his desk from the sidewalk: "Clients tap on the window, and I wave 'em in," he says. "I do about an hour and a half of legal work a day that I don't bill for. Clients wander in with a document they don't understand, or a question . . . that wouldn't happen in the city. It's casual.

"But if you're not good here, or not fair," he says, "you won't last. The biggest misapprehension city people have is 'the dumb farmer.' He isn't, believe me! If he works, say, 200 acres, you're talking about an operation of $200,000 in real estate and another $100,000 in machinery, most of it probably paid for. He's an astute businessman. Usually he's scrupulously honest and easy to get along with—a small community obliges both. Things may seem calm here, but the work ethic is very much in effect."

McLean maintains, however, that he will "never grow rich in Exeter as a lawyer."

What's rich, though? McLean and his wife, Rena, go on week-long holidays outside Canada about every four months—England, Florida, Las Vegas, Puerto Rico. Their children—Robin, seven, Jenny, three and Ian, five—are still too young to come along on these trips. They live in a 99-year-old house on a third-acre lot bought for $68,000 two years ago and with self-improvements, he estimates it's now worth $75,000. In a large city, McLean guesses, it would be valued at $150,000. His house has a pool, a sauna, and a poolroom downstairs. Their car is driven about 11,000 miles a year, two-thirds of it on business. In town it isn't used at all, says McLean. If they lived in the city, he says, the family would need two cars. Fresh meat, eggs, fruit and vegetables come cheaper and, because of farmer friends, often as gifts. And there's a saving on clothes. McLean wears a suit and tie only to court; the rest of the time, at the office and at home, it's jeans and sportshirts.

"I admit I'm probably less formal than a lot of small town lawyers," he says. "At first I wore my three-piece suit, but then a farmer comes in with manure on his boots . . . you dress up for a reason; it doesn't add anything here."

McLean is hard-pressed to discuss the negative aspects of small town living. "It would be ludicrous to say we aren't happy," says McLean. "It's quiet, sure. But I recommend it to anyone. We don't miss the 'throb' of the city. Once in a while we go down to Toronto for a few days, and then we really *do* things—see a play, a baseball game, go pub-hopping."

But he will say that he encounters more conflicts of interest in his work than he would in the city; the municipality vs. an individual client, the new plaza vs. a single merchant. He then advises one of the parties to get another lawyer. It's that simple. Rena, he says, misses not being able to walk along Main Street *anonymously*, like she could in Toronto. And yes, sometimes all the gossip gets a bit annoying. There's a saying in Exeter: if you haven't heard a rumour by 10 in the morning, you start one.

"Sure, there's *sometimes* some snub, some of that country hick feeling," continues McLean, "when you meet a Bay Street lawyer. He can't identify with a farm lease. But most of my friends in Toronto envy our situation.

"And where else but in a small town," he says, "would a neighbour stop on a late afternoon and say, 'Doing anything?' and you say no, and he says, 'Come on, then.' "And next thing you know, you're out in a field with a hundred elastic bands around your wrist, bent over tying leaves around cauliflowers. And a bit farther up, the guy's doctor is doing the same. That's *real.* The kids are exposed to farm life every day. They learn things they never would in the city."

Simple pleasures, to be sure. But would an offer from a large Bay Street law firm—and a hefty salary to go with it—prompt him to move back to the city?

His reply comes quickly. "Hell, no."

Chartered accountant Gerald Merner, 33, writes down one, two, three on a pale green pad on his desk. "There are three questions you have to ask yourself about living in a place like Exeter," he says.

"One, do you want to help clients or *people*? Two, do you really like the nice, quiet life? Three, do you think $25,000 to $30,000 is enough to live on? They were all yes for me."

Merner had already had a taste of big city living before he and his family settled in Exeter. After graduating from Ryerson Polytechnical Institute in 1967, he spent five years apprenticing with Thorne Riddell & Co. Today, he is self-employed and advises a total of 300 clients.

But he freely admits that if he had stayed in Toronto he would probably be a junior partner by now in a large firm earning $35,000 a year. In Exeter, he makes $28,000. "But that $7,000 is just the extra I'd need to live in the city. If our grocery bill is $35 a week here, it's $100 there. We freeze and we preserve. We haven't bought any vegetables since June. We get it all free from my father's farm. (Merner's father lives outside of Zurich, a town 10 miles away from Exeter.) Also, I figure I save about $1,000 a year because I don't have to buy so many suits and ties. I don't wear them often.

"In the city," continues Merner, "I wouldn't be on friendly terms with more than 10 percent of the 300-odd clients I might have. Here it's at least 75 percent. I like that. They are all *people* to me.

"Trust may take a few years to build in a place like this; never underestimate the small town businessman. He's a very shrewd, gutsy individual. Here, one unhappy client can just about nullify 100 happy ones. But once you have this trust—it's forever. It's friendship. You curl with the father and maybe coach the son in baseball. You ease the tax load from cradle to grave. And the work is much more diversified. Besides being an auditor-accountant, I'm an appraiser, a management consultant, a tax adviser and a financial counselor."

Merner works out of his five-bedroom house a half-mile from the fifth hole of the Exeter Ironwood Golf Course. His home is worth $66,000, he says, but would probably cost $135,000 in the city. "If I was in Toronto," he says, "I'd spend at least 40 minutes a day commuting. And I'd never have lunch with the kids every day. They are perhaps the biggest reason for living here. Stephen is 12 and Julia, five. They've got hockey, baseball, tennis, ballet, figure skating, lots of free space, the woods and the lake, and there's almost no crime."

Would he return to the city? "It's tempting," he says, "but not likely. I really want to raise the kids here. Besides, I'm going to try for semi-retirement at 40. I own another house here, worth about $45,000, and this one. My Dad's place is worth about $200,000, and he'll take a decent price for it by then—I'll own three self-paying properties. Nice nest eggs for the children too. I'll keep maybe 30 clients—and take it easy. I'm no workaholic!"

"There's one drawback to a small town," says Dr. William Steciuk, 31. "The doctor-patient relationship can easily turn into something more. You meet patients at dances, curling matches, hockey games. Before you know it, you're friends. That can be a hindrance. I prefer to keep my emotional detachment. It's like treating your own child."

Born and raised in Toronto, Dr. Steciuk graduated from the University of Western Ontario, in London, in 1975. His wife, Sharon, an elementary school teacher, supported him through school. "London was saturated with doctors," he says. "We loved the country up here, so we came out. It's a good place to work. There's all the backup help I need as close as London.

"As a physician you have more respect, you're looked up to more here than in the city. You have a slightly higher profile. I shouldn't maybe, but I like that. More doors are open to us. We function at more levels—farmers, businessmen, other professionals."

Dr. Steciuk's annual income is more than $46,661, the professional average. (He won't say exactly how much he currently earns, however.) When he first came to Exeter in 1976, he rented a house while one was being built for him in Grand Bend on Lake Huron. This house, which has a market value of $70,000, is now completed. But Dr. Steciuk is building a new house, worth $80,000, closer to Exeter because he finds the 30-mile daily drive too time-consuming.

The Steciuks take three to four one-week holidays a year to the Barbados, Nevada, Haiti. In winter, they ski every weekend at Collingwood, 150 miles away. Like Keith McLean and Gerald Merner, Dr. Steciuk likes to have lunch every day with his children, Freddie, four and Susan, two.

Dr. Steciuk finds there isn't much difference, between a small town and the big city, in the types of ailments he's asked to treat. Surprisingly, he says, he encounters anxieties and depressions that result from tension just as much in Exeter as in London. As a result, he often finds himself doing more reassuring than healing. It is rare, he maintains, for anyone in town to try and put one over on him, say, in getting a prescription.

Lest reruns of *The Waltons* inspire misconceptions, however, Dr. Steciuk says that the image of the country doctor, the one who visits patients at home at all hours and in all weather, is almost a figure of the past. His own practice is an "appointment trade." Still, in a small town, he says, "you're always the doctor. You walk in a grocery store, somebody spots you, shows you a cut thumb, and says, 'You think I need this stitched, doc?' Or, 'You're just the guy I wanted to see. How's my X-ray?' Sometimes, this is a bit annoying. It wouldn't happen in the city. But you get used to it."

Although Dr. Steciuk says he would look closely at moving to the city if an offer promised a tripled income, he doesn't want to live in the United States nor does he wish to live in a cosmopolitan centre. “I plan,” he says, “to spend the rest of my practising career in Exeter.”

That impression of tranquillity, curious in men so young, is there because they say they have no major goals to work toward. Their lives are rich, their goals satisfied, their futures optimistic both professionally and personally. They are not wanting.

They have found the good life.

19. Explorer-Poet of the Last Frontier (1980)

Right now, in March, Fred Bruemmer is out on the ice by the Magdalen Islands in the Gulf of St. Lawrence photographing harp seals. It's his 14th trip, but he'll stay two or three weeks because, he says, "I enjoy their beauty." Yet he already has 10,000 pictures of the beasts, has written a dozen articles on them and, in 1977, published a book, *The Life of the Harp Seal.* "But that's all incidental," he explains, "just an outgrowth, a byproduct of what I simply like doing." And *that,* he says, is "trundling off to distant, isolated places and looking at plants and animals and people." Bruemmer isn't always so concise—in his quiet way he loves to talk—but that's how he can sum up the why and the what of his life. And it's true. His life is geared precisely to his specification—to do what he likes; but the "byproduct" is not as "incidental" as he makes out. It has made him, slowly and without fanfare, one of the least-known world-famous men in Canada.

Three weeks on the Magdalens is a run around the block for Bruemmer. Usually the 50-year-old writer-photographer is gone from his Montreal home six months of the year, thousands of miles away up in the Arctic. For 18 years he has roamed from the islands off Siberia, across Alaska, Canada, Greenland, as far east as Lapland—though you would never guess it in meeting him. "I disappoint people at first," he admits. "They think, 'He must make up those stories.'" Tall, gangly, pale-faced and bald, he just doesn't look like an Arctic explorer. Still, in miles travelled he easily equals Arctic greats Rasmussen, Stefansson, Nansen, Peary and Freuchen; in intensity of experience he may have surpassed them; and in talent for sharing that experience—the "incidental" stuff—Bruemmer is in a class by himself. Since launching his freelance career in '63, the Latvian-born high-school dropout has written seven books on the North—finishing the last one two weeks ago—and about 500 magazine articles. The books are sold in more than a dozen countries; some are translated into French and German and will soon be available in the Scandinavian languages and in Dutch. The articles run in mass-circulation publications—the old *Weekend Magazine* and Quebec's *Perspectives* gave him his start—and in such respected journals as *Natural History, Audubon Magazine* and *International Wildlife.* This awesome output, all done, of course, between trips, has earned Bruemmer a reputation as the foremost interpreter of the Arctic in the world.

William Taylor, director of Ottawa's National Museum of Man and an expert on the North, calls Bruemmer's *The Arctic* (1975) "the most comprehensive single book on its subject matter ever presented." Even more telling, the Inuit themselves see Bruemmer as their Boswell: his books are used in schools throughout the North telling children of the culture that was theirs. From his journeys Bruemmer has brought back 140,000 pictures and some 20,000 pages of meticulous notes. It's a unique and irreplaceable record because what he witnessed was a culture dying. Nine years ago he wrote *Seasons of the Eskimo,* subtitled *A Vanishing Way of Life*. That life *has* now vanished. What he saw will not be seen again. And he still has much to tell.

This winter Bruemmer told a lot; his sixth book, *Children of the North,* appeared in November; his seventh, a book for children, tentatively called *Bear River,* will be at the International Children's Book Fair in Bologna, Italy, this month and is due in September; a one-man showing of his photographs ran in Toronto and in London, Ontario, where it closed last month; and he wrote 16 articles totaling 50,000 words.

Much like the traditional Inuit, Bruemmer thinks of time in seasons. Winter is when he's home working. Home is with Maud, his wife, and Aurel, 17, and René, 12, in a modest house on a quiet street. Work is writing—in longhand, 10 hours a day, seven days a week, until a project is done. And also in winter are breaks for dining out, movies, the opera. But not many.

Spring, summer and fall are for travelling. Little planning goes into the journeys. "I land and play it by ear," says Bruemmer. Much of the time, he moves around very little, spending weeks alone on an island "shooting" flowers, or living for three, five, eight months in the same Inuit camp. Coming up now are trips to Alaska, to watch sea lions, and to the Central Arctic for a stay with an Inuit family. He has done it all before but, he says, "It's never the same. I'm always learning. There are 55 academic disciplines in the Arctic jigsaw puzzle. . . . And there's a pleasure in taking good pictures. Last fall I was up in a 12-foot tower near Churchill shooting polar bears. They wait for freeze-up to go hunting on Hudson Bay. In two weeks we had one sunny day and I caught a bear against the sunset, all black, his fur like a golden halo. . . . And there are primitive joys. For five days and nights six of us sat on a little island with no food. Finally we caught a one and a half pound white fish. We cut it in six and ate it, guts, scales and all, *tout de suite*. Terrific! And the adrenalin rushing in time of danger—and afterwards the exhilaration. You won! You against . . ."

Bruemmer thought a moment: "In '71, off the coast of Greenland, coming back from a walrus hunt, the others in kayaks ahead and out of sight. I'm in a rowboat because of the cameras, and it's now full of dead walrus. I've been rowing for 20 hours. Hands blistered, arms sore. An iceberg juts out from an island it's drifted against. It must be 20 storeys high. As I pass beneath, the thing moans and starts to keel over slowly. The sun has melted a lake on top. Wind is moving the water and that's causing the iceberg to topple—on *me*. God knows where the power comes from, but I *shoot* through the sea. I row, row, and row. I have to get at least a mile away not to get sucked under if the iceberg falls over. It moans louder and keeps tipping further and further. I *row*. And then water, first a bit, then tons of it comes plunging down over the lake edge on top. And slowly, slowly, moaning and cracking, the iceberg rights itself. I am a mile away, all alone, laughing like a demon."

Bruemmer says he now has the best of two worlds. "There's the hardship and excitement up north, and a very contented, sedentary life at home. It's a happy combination. I do what I like best and I make a living at it."

It wasn't always so. Somewhere in *Seasons* it says: "To endure and succeed in such a life, a hunter must be resourceful and hardy, he must have faith in himself, a lot of optimism, a certain fatalism, and the ability to live each day and enjoy the good it brings and not spoil it with worry about the morrow." That goes for a freelancer's risky life as well. Bruemmer was 33, married two years and a father when he went on his own. He had four years' experience as a reporter on two small-town papers in Ontario and the Montreal *Gazette*. He had wandered about Europe, North Africa and the Middle East for six years earning his way with short features for Canadian papers and a French animal magazine. Perhaps the most important thing he learned then was how to live and travel cheaply. This was just as well, because in his first year of freelancing he made $900 and it took seven years to clear $10,000. They were lean years, made all the rougher by Bruemmer's unheard-of credo never to accept assignments. His way is to mail text and picture packages to editors on a take-it or leave-it basis. "The reason is I'd feel responsible to someone else," he explains. "I'd be taking money in advance for something I couldn't be sure would come out right." He stresses that he certainly would have had to skulk back into harness were it not for his wife. Born and raised in Indonesia, the dark, attractive Maud accepted, supported, and somehow ran the house. Her reasoning isn't complicated: "Fred has to do what he has to do."

And do it Fred's way. "What I treasure most is independence," he says. And singlemindedly he and Maud have shaped their life to where they have more of it than most. They now could live off his "capital," the pictures and notes of which less than five per cent have been used in what he has published so far. No more arduous journeys; stay home and write. But Maud says, "Fred will go back up there as long as he can crawl."

Bruemmer's passion blossomed soon after he came to Canada in 1950 to work in the mines at Kirkland Lake, Ontario. Behind him were the Second

World War, the death of his parents and 18 months in a Russian prison camp. (Maud spent three and a half years in a Japanese prison camp.) "I remember everybody in town went south for their holidays," he says. "I bought a motorcycle and explored the bush roads. I made a trip to James Bay—and that was *it*. The timelessness, the space, the freedom. I walk and walk up North. I'm fascinated by nature and by people closely bound to it.

"I get along fine with the Inuit because I accept them as they are. In the humblest way I ask, 'May I join you?' I've learned to be a very minor nuisance. I'm patient. The first question is always, 'Will you eat our food?' Where I go it's traditional—seal, ducks, eggs, caribou and fish, often raw. I like it. Soon the awkwardness wears off. I'm a *kabloona* [white man] with no complaints, advice or questions."

Bruemmer is angry in a sad and fatalistic way. "*Children* isn't a happy book," he says. "It shows the end result of a culture in decay. Famine, infanticide, the death of the old people, that's all gone. But the drink problem is catastrophic, and the suicide rate is horrible. The old life was hard, but emotionally it was more secure. We tried to make whites of them in one generation.

"An archeologist at Lake Harbor once showed me a campsite where four or five families, 25 people at most, had lived continually for 4,000 years—longer than Rome or Babylon. It was one of the most specialized and static cultures there's ever been. Its only materials were bone, stone, ivory, baleen, ice, snow, hides. . . . I have no sense of mission at all, but somebody had to do what I've done. So much would have been lost otherwise."

Bruemmer may be accepted as a harmless *kabloona,* but he's still thought odd. For instance, back after a hunt of, say, two days and nights when everybody is full of meat and tea and fast asleep, Bruemmer might still be sitting upright, scribbling. When the weather is foul that's *all* he does. Often he's talking to himself:

. . . we cut up the seal, ate part of the guts, together with chips of raw blubber and liver. We were a sight sitting over that pile of intestines, hands and faces covered with blood, gorging ourselves. It's rather primeval. Still, why not?

I got lost. It rained, it was foggy, and I took a wrong turn by the coast. . . . Got here by 11 p.m. How little it takes to be happy. Food, a dry tent and not being lost at night in the Arctic.

. . . the weather is beastly, cold, windy and raw, snow drifting, and bleak, bleak, bleak. Arctic spring!

In different words this message occurs again and again:

You're the outsider here, don't complain. If you don't like it, stay away. Cheer up, you bastard!

And then the *kabloona*'s endless walks. Cameras around his neck, he wanders off for hours, even days. But that's his way, is how his Inuit hosts react. Sometimes they refer to him, though, as a wolf, a lone wolf. And they are right. He lives with them but, finally, he's not one of them; they remain separate entities. And back in the South—who has seen what he has seen? But he wants to share. So he sits in his workroom, writing—which really is being alone. The room is bare of decorations, except for a poster-size colour print of a wolf on a hill of snow at night.

20. The Little Shop on Main Street (1981)

Everybody in Knox Variety hears them—the magazine readers, greeting-card browsers, pop drinkers, the woman turning the rack with pantyhose, the people lined up at the post office in back.

"They're stale, Mr. Knox," says one and holds high an open bag of potato chips.

"Stale, Mr. Knox," echoes her friend helpfully.

Their voices penetrate to every corner of the cluttered little store. Only Bill Knox, right in front of them, doesn't seem to hear. The portly, 68-year-old proprietor is taking stock of his cigarettes, adding up how many packs are left of a certain brand. If he stops now, he'll lose track.

"Mr. Knox?"

Stocktaking is a never-ending chore in this miniature Eaton's. Knox, his wife, Mary, and their eldest daughter, Diane Malinksy, who run the store in shifts, are at it continually. Magazines take four hours a week, toys and drugs an hour, soft drinks 1½ hours, cigarettes five hours. Cigarettes are crucial because they are the biggest seller.

Knox's is on Main Street in the upper Beaches district, an enclave of small-town living in Toronto's east end. Downtown, there, seems far away. It's a good location, across from a public school and a hockey arena. But once there were four other enterprises like it nearby. Now only one besides Knox's is left. The chain stores have moved in. Look around any urban neighbourhood in Canada and see how many longtime, family-owned variety stores still survive. For Bill Knox to run out of one particular brand of cigarettes is unthinkable.

"Mr. Knox!"

As it is, the store has to stay open six days from 8 a.m. to 11 p.m., Sundays from 11 a.m. to 10 p.m. When one of the three is sick, the others split that shift. When Mary isn't working, she's home doing the books. Saturday night, when a part-timer helps out, is the only night Bill and Mary Knox are off together. Two children—and their husbands, four grandchildren, gardening, a little TV—but it's Knox Variety that consumes their life.

"Mr. Knox!"

Knox finishes the count and in red ballpoint enters a figure on the stock sheet; finicky, he retraces the number. Then he turns to the girls. He looks from one to the other, cool, businesslike. "You said stale?"

"Yes, Mr. Knox."

"Yeah!"

Knox has a tiny white moustache and is nearly bald. He is dressed in creaseless trousers, an open sport shirt and a tired cardigan. Stale chips are not good news. He shakes his head. "Stale, huh?"

"Yes, honest."

This is a serious complaint. It's a problem to tackle with patience, caution—and a touch of skepticism. For 27 years, after all, youngsters have marched in and made similar wild claims. Sure, the store needs a dusting, a wash, a coat of paint, new carpeting. The turquoise walls, yellowish neon light and filmed-over windows give a feeling of being inside an aquarium. But judge not on appearances—Knox Variety gives honest value. Stale chips are a gyp, and the absolute rule here is: *Never* gyp.

It isn't as if temptation doesn't occur occasionally. A kid will come in, for instance, waving a $5, a $10, even a $20 bill. "How much candy can I get for this?" he'll say. Taking the bill, Knox will say, "I'll keep this. You tell your Mom to call me." To do otherwise would constitute a gyp, according to Knox. Most times, of course, the money's been pinched from Ma's purse. As it is, Knox feels that selling some of his merchandise is almost a gyp, the quality is so poor. "Everything's going down," he says. "Customers pay for packaging. I'm actually ashamed of some of this stuff, like the toys."

"They can't be stale."

"Honest!"

"But I only got 'em in yesterday."

There's an impasse. Knox can say go away or give in. But that's not how it's done. "We built this business on children," he says. "Now *their* children come in, even their grandchildren. I see some of these kids every day. They are customers. Anyhow, I like kids. I like 'em better than adults."

That isn't easy to tell. Usually, the taciturn Knox is strictly business with everybody, big and little. This is about as funny as he gets: "I'm my own boss. Only my customers and the government can tell me what to do.

"I look stern and people tend to shy off," he says. "I can't play-act. Mary calls me a sourpuss." Certainly his slim and energetic wife is friendly enough and Diane takes after her mother. It's because of those two that customers on vacation mail cards to the store or stop in with good-time wishes before a holiday. Knox claims Mary knows all the customers by name, knows their families, knows their troubles. "Meeting people," she explains, "is what I like best. It's what keeps me going."

"Taste 'em then, Mr. Knox."

Knox sighs. He picks a chip out of the bag, looks at it, bites it, chews it, frowns. It's stale. "You're right. Get another bag."

* * * * *

The mark-up on a 35-cent bag of chips is seven cents—therefore the caution. Knox's is a penny operation. And, says the owner, while the turnover may be three or four times what it was 27 years ago, it is increasingly difficult to scrape enough pennies together. Rent, for instance, was once $75 a month for the 35-by-70-foot space; now it's $400.

The squeeze is on in many ways. Some random examples: Knox has always sold bread. One day the breadman said he couldn't deliver anymore without a minimum weekly guarantee of $125 in sales. Knox couldn't promise and was promptly cut off. Knox stocks some 350 magazine titles, or $2,000 worth. They used to be delivered free, now he pays $1.75 per drop. Soft-drink dealers pressure him to stock more than he needs by his own reckoning, or risk suddenly being without. Some soft-drink companies, these days, will first supply a huge operation such as Toronto's Canadian National Exhibition, for instance, to the detriment—in the hot days of August—of a steady but small customer such as Knox. As a convenience for shoppers, Knox has always had a payphone in the store. It used to earn him a small kick-back. Today he must pay Bell Canada $3.60 a month plus the difference if the phone has not taken in the company-set monthly quota in dimes. And so it goes.

The root cause of the trouble, however, the dreaded enemy, is the chain stores. Efficient, bright, clean and entirely profit-oriented, they seem invincible. It's simple. Chains can buy in bulk at lower prices—food products, giftware, cosmetics, rubber ducks, whatever—and sell cheaper. "I advise anybody going into the variety business: 'Don't. The little guy is dead.'"

Thus another small, old way of life in Canada inexorably fades away. Most of us raised in a city or town recall a close connection with the neighborhood variety store. It was a wondrous place that held, when you were little, just about everything in the world you might want—toys, comic books, dolls, knives and, above all, marvellous things to eat, drink and chew that were bad for you. It was probably there where you first seriously learned to want.

Always open, it was the only store where you really felt welcome. Even the dog was. Mary Knox remembers Boots, a black Labrador that trotted in most mornings for at least 10 years for a chocolate fudge square. It was the place to spend allowance and chore-earnings. The owner was like an indulging older friend, shooing you out in time for school or supper; later, selling you cigarettes but sorry you had started smoking. Even broke, you dropped in just to look around.

On a recent rainy morning at Knox's, a woman came in with a tot on either hand. Slowly the three wandered around. The children pointed and the woman explained—key rings, dart boards, the bubble-gum machine, sunglasses, plastic clarinets and hair curlers. The tour lasted nearly an hour. Nothing was purchased.

As the potato chip girls leave and several adult customers move up, Bill Knox sinks below the candy counter. It's open on his side, and the shelves hold shallow cartons filled with brilliantly colored candies. They cost one, two, three or five cents. Most popular are the one-centres. Knox's candyman warned recently that the one-centres were going to be phased out—two one-cent candies for three cents, three one-centres for five cents. A dark sign of the times. But Knox remembers with a rare, small smile, "The candy companies tried that stunt two years ago—and got nowhere. The kids wouldn't buy 'em."

Hidden from sight, on one knee, Knox attends three silent patrons. Each opens a fist. "Seven cents," he says. Their eyes move slowly over the candies.

"Well, you pick 'em," says Knox, shifting his weight. He has gained a lot since he quit smoking last August.

"How about the orange ones?"

Also, he has not given up his after-work beer at the Benlamond. He drops in at "the Benny" when he's done at 2 p.m. and again with Mary at 11, when she's locked up.

"The yellow ones?"

The store, the Benny and home are the three points of an even-sided triangle in which Knox lives his life; each is about a four-minute drive from the other. Last summer, on a whim and after 20 years, Knox took a streetcar downtown. Only Simpsons and Old City Hall were familiar. "It was like being in a foreign country."

A finger points at the jujubes, but is unsure.

"No, eh?"

It points at the strawberries.

"Okay," says Knox and lifts one out.

Next is a black baby.

"Okay . . ."

A cream square.

"Okay."

Now a jujube.

"Okay. You got two cents left."

Fingers point at green leaves, jelly beans, cherries.

"Two cents, I said."

A jelly bean and a cherry, then.

"Okay. That's it. Thank you."

"I want a bag, Mr. Knox," pipes up one of the three.

"You can't have a bag. Put 'em in your pocket."

The first of the waiting adults needs string to tie up newspapers and a bicycle-tire repair kit. A second wants a pocket notebook and thumbtacks. A third asks for a certain fabric dye. Their faintly surprised reaction that the items are in stock is a common one. A fourth buys $45 of lottery tickets.

"Lotteries gave us a big lift," says Knox. "They pay the rent." Depending on the lottery, he earns from five to eight percent of the price of a ticket, and a kickback of one to five percent on the spoils of a winner. On pre-draw days gamblers crowd the store. The Knoxes each buy a Lottario ticket based on the birth dates of their grandchildren every week. Once they won $1,000. Alice Missons, who has run the post office for Knox since it started 12 years ago and still calls him Mr. Knox, has $1,300 saved in winnings. She plans to buy a boat for her husband who loves fishing. The post office is a happy plus for Knox. In summer, the commission may go to $300 a month; at Christmas, up to $900.

And so the day goes. Adults and children. Balloons, nail polish, screwdrivers, puzzles and Band-Aids. The soft-drink and ice-cream coolers hum; the radio sings. Rarely is the place empty. "You can't get rich," says Knox, "but this is my business and my recreation. I'll never retire. I've gone in sick. I'll come in early on a Sunday. I like every part of the work." If he had to do it over, he wouldn't change much.

Knox was born in Sydney Mines, near Sydney, N.S. The family settled in Toronto shortly after World War I. His father, a veteran with a silver plate in his head, found work in Simpsons' china department. At 14, Bill was laying cement sidewalks at $5 for a six-day week. A few years later he, too, joined the china department.

He met Mary there and after a two-year engagement they were married on Jan. 22, 1937. It was Friday. Payday. Though both still lived at home, they had decided to get it over with quietly and tell their families next day. The ceremony was witnessed in a minister's home by a married couple from work. Afterwards the four blew Bill's weekly salary of $12.50 on a meal in a restaurant. Around midnight the newlyweds arrived at the three-bedroom Knox home. Mother, sisters and brother were asleep upstairs; father was downstairs listening to the radio. "My dad was a little bit psychic," recalls Bill. "He said, 'Mary, you wouldn't tell me a lie. Did you and Bill get married?' Mary said, 'Yes.' And Dad woke up everybody to tell 'em. Then Mary went upstairs to sleep in my sisters' room, and I in the boys' room. But guess who was lying next to me in the morning? While I was sleeping, Mother had kicked my brother out. . . ."

Except for army service as a cook during World War II, Knox worked 20 years for Simpsons. His salary in 1954 was $60 a week, but he had $10,000 in the company's profit-sharing plan and bought the store for $8,000. Why a variety store? Because it sold china and Knox knew china. Mary, the bookkeeper, says they now do about $98,000 of business a year; she guesses the store's worth is about $60,000. "We've earned enough," says Knox, "to put food on the table, make payments on the house, run a little car." They now own their two-storey, 100-year-old house, and Mary says the 50-by-50-foot property would probably fetch $100,000. In winter, the couple visits Florida for a month, often taking a grandchild along. In summer, the store closes for two weeks, and Knox goes fishing. Life isn't so bad.

And yet. "When I look back," says Knox quietly, "I see that people have changed for the worse. They don't share as they used to. They don't help. Everybody is out for themself. And people aren't as trustworthy anymore. I used to give a lot of credit. Now there are just two customers who get it. Last Christmas I let a woman have $38 in toys. She'd been coming in for years. 'I'll pay you back,' she said. I never saw her again. . . . I almost never take post-dated cheques. They bounce. It isn't the money. It's the broken faith.

"I used to think there were more good people than bad. Now I think more are going sour. Especially kids. There isn't the upbringing. Mothers used to make lunches. Now they give the kids a couple of dollars and they spend 'em here on pop and candy. Parents don't seem to care. Kids used to be mischievous. One little beggar poured detergent in my pop cooler. It ran on rotating water then. The whole place full of suds and me cleaning till 4 a.m. Had it out with the boy, and he promised to be good. Then he fixed the lock on the front door so customers were shut out. You couldn't help liking him, though. These days kids are hurtful. And they steal. And adults steal."

Knox figures he loses about $2,000 in stolen merchandise a year. There isn't much he can do. "It goes on all the time," he says. "You get used to it." Catching the odd fellow with "girlie" magazines in a folded newspaper under his arm is mostly luck. While one teenager makes a legitimate purchase, others are free to make their moves. Knox has even had his lunch sandwich stolen out of the fridge. Saddest, perhaps, was the day when he had to put up a string barring easy entry into that special place behind the candy counter. Even though there's nearly always someone by the cash register there, he had begun to miss packs, even cartons, of cigarettes and rolls of change. Only the very tiny now fit under the string.

That's the storekeeper's one big beef—dishonesty. There aren't many others. Credit he doesn't like. For 27 years salesmen have begged him to take credit. "If I can't pay for it," he says, "I don't want it." "Braggarts" he doesn't like. A braggart is "a fellow who thinks he has all the answers." He may have to serve a braggart in the store, but he'll never allow one at his table at the Benny.

Bill and Mary Knox have been coming to the Benny for 35 years. Their corner table overlooks the floor. Waiters hold it for them. On Saturday night they come in about seven. The Benny fills with smoke and noise and it's time to relax.

"We're father and mother to so many people here," says Mary. "They've known us all their lives. We're never bothered. They know we put up with the public all day." Friends come to sit at their table. "Bill liked going for a beer after work," she remembers. "So I figured, 'Me too.' With the first one I held my nose."

Here, too, Bill Knox doesn't speak much. After a while he allows, "I like sitting here. It doesn't take much to entertain me. I can sit here and think about my garden. I can think about my business. I can think about what's happened over the years."

21. Three-Piece Perfection (1982)

The large reception room breathes reserve, tradition, solidity. Very quiet and often empty, it's like the inner sanctum of an establishment club: Only long-time members will feel at ease instantly. It's spacious, brightly lit, high ceilinged. The furniture gleams—leather chairs, burled-walnut tables, walnut shelves showing bolts of cloth, tall mirrors, a glassed-in counter full of ties. The mahogany-panelled walls carry prints of fox hunts and stagecoaches. The room's silence relaxes, soothes.

The building you're in is at the heart of perhaps the most frenetically busy environment in the country. But in this room, haste is unseemly; sudden disruptions, unheard of. Time slows down. A more common mood, probably, in the gentler days of Charles and William, founders of Lloyd Bros. Ltd., "purveyors of fine suitings to gentlemen since 1904." Their sons Charles and Edward, however, preserve it still.

Lloyd's is on the top floor of a seven-storey building on Bay Street in downtown Toronto. It's one of those splendid, old, "gentleman's bespoke" concerns that, notwithstanding mass production and mechanization, stubbornly pursues pure Savile Row tailoring. Except for an occasional brochure for clients, it doesn't advertise.

Two or three minutes go by. Finally, from the back emerge the Lloyd cousins. They often deal together with people. They also do the same work, the crucial measuring, cutting and fitting; neither can sew to save his life, nor could their fathers. They cross the room in unhurried, rolling strides. They both walk like that. Charles is 72, Edward, 62, and some call them Chuck and Ted, nicknames that don't fit. One client fondly describes them as "walking monuments to Victorian dignity." They are tall, trim, grey-haired, impeccably dressed and easily as distinguished-looking as, presumably, their customers. They murmur greetings.

Later, you may realize that in those first few moments the cousins watched you extremely closely. It's a merciless scrutiny that takes in every detail of appearance and manners and deduces in a flash your tastes, habits and financial standing. Accuracy is imperative, obviously. Four good eyes take your measure. It's a singular skill that keeps them at the top of their craft, stalwartly offering hand service in a machine age. Edward allows, "There aren't many of us good guys left." Hardly any, in fact. *Fortune* magazine recently estimated that there are just 15 firms of these "good guys" around the globe.

Lloyd Bros., the oldest and one of the very few Canadian members of the prestigious Custom Tailors and Designers Association of America, is generally considered one of them. The cousins aren't so much taciturn as sparing of words. Small talk is usually kept to a minimum. In undertones—it's how they usually speak; two yards away and you can't hear them—they directly ask after your pleasure. Be calm, deliberate, specific. Feel safe. The cousins aren't *selling*. As another of those illustrious 15, New York's William Fioravanti, said: "A good tailor doesn't go looking for customers; customers go looking for a good tailor." The cousins will *consult* with you on material, colour, style—and on price, if you like. They will offer courtesy, patience, competence, and authority if necessary. You may ask, for instance, for a flap on the breast pocket of the coat of your new dark-blue, three-piece suit. Charles will shake his head and simply say, "It wouldn't do." And he'll be right, of course. However, enjoy the discussion. For a little while "the real you" will be the focus of an attention rarely known before.

A favourite remark around Lloyd's is: "They claim there's never been a perfect suit made yet. We keep trying!" What *does* set a master tailor's work apart? Someone has said that these craftsmen make "garments of secret meaning." But usually they are just business suits, often of extremely conservative cut and hue.

Such a suit is, of course, of good cloth and fits well (head-on *and* in profile). Sleeve buttons actually work, stripes abut exactly from one piece of fabric to the next, belt loop and trouser pleat are perfectly aligned, pockets fit snug to the body, side buckles on vests have hand-sewn eyelets. The suits will artfully drape a paunch or concave chest, or build up shoulders, or hide bow legs. What the suit does not do is "make" the man. Rather, he should look slimmer, straighter, more comfortable—and feel it. But it is the man who should be remembered, not what he wore. Nor who his tailor is, incidentally. That can lead to vulgar speculation as to the cost of what's on one's back. Some Lloyd clients insist on labelless garments. Growls a financier, "It's nobody's goddamn business where I buy my clothes."

Thus, the craftsman's creation does more than serve decoration, modesty, protection. Ralph Waldo Emerson said that awareness of being really well-dressed "gives a feeling of inward tranquillity which religion is powerless to bestow." The chairman of one of the largest industrial concerns in Canada put it less grandly. At every annual meeting he wears a new suit. Afterwards, there's a photograph taken of the board of directors. Every year, on his next visit to Lloyd's, he remarks: "I look at that picture and I remember I just *knew* I was the best-dressed man in the room!"

This "knowing" has over the years attracted a condensed *Who's Who in Canada* of clients, some clients' wives, and on 21st birthdays, clients' sons and sons' sons. The cousins have been in the homes of many of them to give fittings. Three-quarters of the customers, however, are still addressed as "Mister" by the tailors. The wives of about half the clients have a big say in what their men wear. The other half are largely men content to trust the cousins' fairly conservative tastes. Most of the customers have 39- to 40-inch waists. At every fitting, they swear they're coming down to 34. If their tailors were betting men, they'd be rich.

The cousins are very discreet about those they dress. No names. When pressed, they may list some occupations: prime ministers, senators, premiers, symphony conductors, diplomats, authors, scholars, bankers, doctors, lawyers, brokers, newspaper magnates, chief justices, and "a fair parcel of judges." Two-thirds are from Ontario, the rest from across Canada, the northern United States, and even London. Discretion forbids revealing more.

After considerable deliberation, you've picked your cloth and style. Be careful with humour. "Can you make me look like Prince Philip?" for example, may cause really thoughtful looks. That's not a silly question here. The cousins invite you into one of two fitting rooms in the rear of their 2 300-square-foot establishment.

They take 33 measurements. If in some small way you're misshapen, they'll not tell you. Depending on whether the material is in-house or not, the first try-on will be in eight days or two weeks. There may be one or two more fittings; usually just one. A suit takes 36 work-hours to complete. Delivery is in five to six weeks. Don't plead to have it sooner. "We don't," Charles may say gently, "put it through a meat-grinder, you know."

Charles will set to work first, translating your dimensions with copper-tipped rulers and wax chalk onto heavy-weight wrapping paper. He cuts the pattern with foot-long scissors. With the pieces of paper pinned to the 3½ running yards of your cloth, Edward "chops" the coat and vest; Charles, the trousers. Next, the swathes of fabric are distributed in the sewing room. There, sewing machines whir, scissors snip, and irons thump worktables, pressing cloth flat. The cousins say they've been very lucky with their staff, most of whom have worked for Lloyd's for 25 years or more. There are six jacket specialists, two trouser experts and 75-year-old Sigmund Meisenberger, the only full-time vest man left in the land. They will baste your suit together in big white stitches for the first try-on.

*****

Two weeks have passed. You've returned for the all-important, first try-on. The Lloyd cousins say they like this part of the job best. *The Modern Tailor, Outfitter and Clothier*, a three-volume work published in Britain in 1928, explains what happens. "The try-on stage provides an occasion for the free and fruitful discussion of general design, distinctive details, fashionable features, becoming effects, artistic values and personal preferences, when any, or all, may be adjusted or readjusted.

"It is beyond the power of the most experienced cutter to gather what precisely is in the mind of his customer when measurements are being taken, as it is impossible for the clearest-thinking client to explain at that time what he, or she, desires in every detail. But before the mirrors of the fitting-room, fancies take shape, wishes leap into expression, errors of judgment or understanding are revealed, just when such difficulties . . . can be defeated by competent craftsmanship and cheerful courage."

So you pose and ponder in front of the mirror, as you and the cousins examine and re-examine the effect, until it "feels" perfect. After this session (sometimes there's one more before the cousins are satisfied), your suit will be "rebasted"—ripped apart and sewn together again from scratch, but this time with exquisite care, incorporating every detail. "We're different from a factory," says foreman Archimede di Biagio, "because we control the stitches—one by one." Edward says the suit will end up "lasting longer and finishing stronger." And that, together with looks and that sense of well-being, is what you'll pay for.

Money. Maybe you've discussed it, maybe not. Do people talk cost in a Rolls-Royce showroom? The cousins say two or three new garments a year keep anybody's wardrobe in shape. Some clients order six suits a year, some 12, some 20 and some 26. In 1904, a Lloyd suit cost $30. Today, they *start* at $750 ($825 with vest). Trousers are $190, sport coats $550, shirts $75 (not made on the premises), topcoats $700, overcoats $850, and dinner suits $850. A suit in fine wool goes for $1,145, a camel's-hair coat for $1,600. Lloyd's makes about 600 suits a year.

Edward suggests that the basic wardrobe for a young man starting out in business might consist of: nine suits, two sport coats, four pairs of trousers, one topcoat, one overcoat, one dinner suit, 12 shirts and 25 ties (at $20 each). That's $12,410 ($675 extra with vests). Considering that kind of outlay, durability is critically important, if you appreciate value for your money. "The minimum life of one of our suits is four years," Edward attests.

It would be nice to hear some clients speak to this effect. The cousins relent and, with the permission of the owners of some of their garments, reveal three names. Says Donald Simon, professor of business at Toronto's Ryerson Polytechnical Institute: "I don't have to waste time shopping. Lloyd's clothes last me for years." John A. Rhind, chairman of the board and chief executive officer of the Confederation Life Insurance Company, recalls his father saying, over 40 years ago, that he had only one complaint about Lloyd's: "Their suits never wear out." And A. Gordon Cardy, chairman of the board and president of Canadian Pacific Hotels, recalls: "At a dinner recently, the fellow next to me said, 'Nice suit!' 'Thanks,' I said. 'Just new, eh?' he said. 'No,' I said, 'It's from '71.'"

Simon is "apprehensive about what's going to happen with Lloyd's in the future." None of the cousins' children will be following in the business. Charles was 23 when he joined the firm. He can remember in the '20s and '30s that the three blocks along Bay between King and York streets were nearly solid with custom tailors. "It was like Savile Row," he says. "Most were family businesses. The sons didn't want to go in, and so they died out. We're the only ones left." Which is sad, somehow.

Finally, the big day arrives. Your suit is ready. Charles and Edward move around you, step away, kneel. They tug at the suit, flatten it, straighten it. They tell you to hoist the pants, stand up straight, turn around. They're like nervous fathers. They back away, looking.

"I think you'll like it," Charles allows at last.

"It's perfect!" you say.

"I guess we were lucky," Edward murmurs.

22. Going Out in Style (1986)

One evening about 52 years ago, in his home in the little town of Modica on the island of Sicily, Constable Giorgio Buscema said to Francesco, the third-eldest of his six children, "So, have you decided?" The answer had always been no before. There was, after all, still a year to go before Francesco turned nine. But to his surprise, the little boy said, "Yes, Papa."

"You have? Are you sure?"

"Yes, Papa."

"Well?"

"I want to be a barber."

Frank Buscema, at 60 the dark-eyed, dark-moustached owner of The Little Barber Shop at the corner of Kingston and Kingswood roads in Toronto's east end, still recalls his father's response. "A barber! Your brother is a mechanic. . . . Why a barber?"

"I have watched them, Papa. I know I will like cutting. I will like shaving. It is clean work."

As was customary in his country (and still is, he says), boys from working-class families decided between their sixth and ninth year what trade they wanted to take up. But even though this was one of the most important conversations in Frank Buscema's life, he hadn't told the entire truth. Young Frank had observed that men came in the afternoons to the barbershop to talk and smoke and play the mandolin and the guitar. He had at eight committed himself to his profession, starting at once every day as an apprentice to a barber after school and half-days on Saturdays and Sundays, just so he could learn to play music.

And he did. Indeed, so well that later, in the summers after World War II, the boss gave him time off to play the guitar and the mandolin in a cafe on the beach that faced Africa.

But in the meantime, he learned his trade too. Taken on as a "soap boy" at the age of eight, Frank was expected to sweep, dust, help customers with their coats and, standing on tiptoe on a crate, lather their faces ready for the barber's razor. Two or three years later, he was allowed to actually handle a cutting tool. No pay, of course—but he was permitted to keep tips. When war did come and the boss joined the army, Frank, being the eldest in the shop at 14 (he'd quit school the previous year), was put in charge of an eight-year-old soap boy, an 11-year-old "shaver" and another qualified barber, aged 13.

In a voice still resonant with accent, Frank tells this story with relish and the fluency of repetition. That's how it was: Tradition, family, respect and honour pressed one's life into a certain mould. You learned very early how to cut hair and then lived on simply plying and perfecting your trade. In the old country, it's still like that, he claims. But in Canada today, Frank the barber is almost an anachronism.

Frank Buscema came to Canada at 31 in 1957 with his wife, Maria, and their five-year-old daughter, Grace. The first seven years, he worked for others. Then, in 1964, he opened the place on Kingston Road. The three pump-up, red vinyl barber chairs facing the two sinks set in specially built cabinets and counter space topped with the best Arborite money could buy cost $3,500. He took a 10-year, $80-per-month lease on the 8-by-42-foot space. Something nice happened when the lease expired. Because he liked Frank, the well-off owner of the two- storey building that houses the shop, plus a jewelry store and a two-bedroom apartment, declined to raise the rent. In 1977, Frank had a chance to buy the building for $45,000, a steal apparently. Today, it's worth $185,000.

The six-foot barber, whose own dark brown, full head of hair is always immaculately clipped and combed, recalls that in the first two years, eight shops like his on a 10-block stretch of Kingston Road had to close up. He himself only made it because he let his second assistant go. What happened, of course, were the Beatles and long hair. The impact on Western males was enormous and as long-lasting as the effects of John F. Kennedy's rejection of hats and Clark Gable's disdain for undershirts.

Barbers suffered. Customers' visits grew increasingly infrequent or ceased altogether. (Frank at the time warned clients that if they felt they had to wear their hair long, at least they shouldn't wear it long on top. Few listened, and there may be some sweet revenge in the fact that many of those who didn't are now bald.) Many barbers quit. According to the Metropolitan Toronto Licensing Commission, there were 712 licensed barbers in 1982, which by May, 1986, had shrunk to 588. And this trend seems to hold true across the country: In Calgary, for example, the licensing division lists 144 in 1980 and just 118 last year. Frank's guess is that over the years about 70 percent of barbershops have gone under.

Gone under but perhaps resurfaced in a new metamorphosis—as *hair stylists*. Ontario's Ministry of Skills Development says that's the key term now. It reports that there are three categories for a "certificate of qualification" in the hair business: barbers, hairdressers and hair stylists. All three take a basic eight-week course; barbers and hairdressers then each take an eight-week "advanced" course, while hair stylists take both for a total of 24 weeks. Barbers and hairdressers, furthermore, must have 4,500 hours of practical experience; for hair stylists, that's 4,740 hours. In Ontario, in March 1985, there were 31,335 hairdressers who held a certificate, while there were 9,842 stylists and just 4,538 barbers.

Meanwhile, Frank Buscema has survived fairly well it seems. Besides the building on Kingston Road, he also owns his $120,000 home in Scarborough. His income he deems his own affair, but he says $18,000 to $20,000 a year is fair for a barber; $25,000 and over is very, very good. Expenses consist of small items such as laundry (towels and the white jackets and pants the men wear) at $20 per week and sharpening the seven pairs of scissors every three months for $24.50.

Frank survives, presumably, because he is good at what he does and "I'm good at it because I *like* it. After 52 years, I still love the talk, the jokes, the teasing." And because there are still customers—most of them men over 35 (about 10 percent are women)—who want a barber simply to be a barber. Sure, Frank is licensed to style, but most of his clientele want a plain no-nonsense cut, so they can see their ears, feel refreshed, lighter.

He survives because there are still a few men left who don't like compulsory shampoos ("sir, I can't cut you otherwise!"), fancy dos or endless sessions with blow-dryers. They resent the creation of an "image" on their heads, which dissolves after the first shower. They care about what they look like, they just aren't fussy. They've withstood the power of television; the oh-so-casually coiffed actors, athletes, game-show hosts, and newsreaders leave them cold. They shave every day even though Don Johnson of *Miami Vice* does not.

Frank is there because a salesman whose hair he cut on his second day in Canada 29 years ago has never missed his twice-a-month visits. Other such customers drive in from Ajax, Oshawa, Pickering, and Agincourt. They wait their turn staring at the two-foot turtle mounted near the ceiling, the seven calendars, the single spiky houseplant in the window. They listen to CKDS, easy-listening music broadcast from Hamilton.

Twelve years ago, Frank took on as assistant the short and friendly Rocco Altobello, 55, from a village south of Naples, who also learned his trade as a child. While Frank and Rocco like to join conversations, tell stories, offer opinions—both closely follow sports and politics—they are mostly expert listeners with fine memories. They remember marriages, births, illnesses, new homes and cars, promotions and vacations.

Finally, Frank earns a living because some clients would rather pay $6.25 for a haircut than fork over a minimum of $12 for a styling. On a busy day, he and Rocco will take care of up to 25 customers. “We spoil ’em, I guess,” he confides. “We get it smooth.” More’s the pity, then, that by year’s end, Frank Buscema will have sold his building and retired.

There’ll be one less red-and-white striped barber pole on the block.

23. Myles to Go (1991)

There was a moment towards the end of dinner with Alannah Myles in Los Angeles when she seemed to trust herself to say something unconsidered.

Not that the strikingly beautiful Canadian rock singer hadn't been spontaneous and candid—but she had been deliberately so. In her energetic, focused way, she had been filtering information about herself since mid-afternoon to convey a particular image, just as she would carefully select the props, clothes, make-up, and hairstyle for a photo shoot; it was a reflex action. Meanwhile, the posh hotel dining room smelt of gardenias; someone was playing piano gently in the lobby. Candlelight made Myles's dark hair shine and turned her pale-green eyes blue. She picked at her fruit salad, sipped her tea. Her voice was slightly hoarse, like that of a smoker and drinker; she's neither. She spoke quickly, forcefully, in little sentences, hurrying and tripping, trying for point and precision, winging from topic to topic. She mentioned her much-loved father, a Toronto businessman, broadcaster, and owner of a once famous watering hole, the Celebrity Club. William Byles (Alannah changed her surname when she turned performer) died in 1989 after eight years of suffering cancer. She referred to him often: he died during the mad days in which she was making her first album. There hadn't been time really to get used to his not being in the world any more. There was a pause. Myles stared in front of her, long hands flat on the table. Then she took a little breath, as if she'd made a decision, and, for once speaking slowly, she said: "You know, when you scrape away all the bullshit—the phone calls, well-wishers, awards, millions of sales, everybody pumping you up and telling you how great you are—what it boils down to is that when I was a little girl all I did was pick up my guitar and play it and let something come through my vocal chords that sounded pleasing and then it became a song. It's the singing—the innocence of it. I become innocent. I do the thing that makes my heart bleed."

The dinner was an unexpected break. From L.A. it had been explained that it wasn't a great time to visit because Myles really wasn't in "promo mode," there being no "new product" (i.e., her second album wasn't ready yet). Still, there was permission to come to an afternoon's rehearsal and the promise of a chat. An entire meal together after the rehearsal meant close-up time in star presence. (We do long for stars in this country, stars we can call our own; the ones we have are so well worn. A new star bursts forth, glittering, preening, marvellously self-absorbed.)

Myles has been a "star" for only two years. Now in her early thirties (her age is secret: "I won't be judged by a number!"), she calls herself "a woman who sings rock 'n' roll, not a rock 'n' roll babe." She was born on Christmas Day in Toronto and raised there and on a ranch near Peterborough, Ontario. When her breakthrough came, after ten years of industry rejection, it was phenomenal.

Suddenly the picture of a defiantly come-hither Myles, her mouth a red gash, was everywhere. The debut album, *Alannah Myles*, sold one million copies in Canada and another four million around the world. (She's signed up for six more with Atlantic Records of New York.) At last year's Juno Awards in Vancouver she gathered five prizes including Album of the Year, Single of the Year ("Black Velvet"), and Most Promising Female Vocalist. In London Myles received the first International Rock Award for Best New Artist. And this year at the Grammy Awards she was named Best Rock Female Vocalist. "Like a storm" was how she described it.

Slim and intense, she's adamant she always knew success would come. Longtime friends concur that this conviction never faltered; a few faithfuls also shared it. Some people, though, saw her self-confidence as just plain brash noisy arrogance. And maybe there was some of that: the unshakable belief in herself was for a long time practically the substance of her. She was a person who said she was going to be a star. "Big strong egos like me end up in this profession. There was all that rejection, but I never, never let myself be a queen of doom.

"I try to convey something basic and simple and earthy—and that's what people respond to . . . like the soldiers in the Gulf." She has a file of short, very polite letters from them. A marine wrote, "Your lyrics and soothing voice accompanied me into the bunkers during SCUD missile attacks and on security patrols." That one hangs framed in her new home in Pacific Palisades.

Myles clung with obsessive tenacity to her fabulous dream, the stock movie dream of the long hard climb to stardom. She lived inside that movie for a big part of her life until, one day, it ran out of script. There she was suddenly on the mountain top, with her album selling like crazy, performing 400 shows in 18 months across Canada, the United States, Europe, Australia, New Zealand, and Japan, being filmed for videos, endlessly interviewed, written to by thousands in 53 countries, heaped with accolades, and, yes, even falling in love. And then, crash, she was in bed in West Hollywood's Sunset Marquis Hotel last November, stressed out, weeping, not eating. She stayed for weeks; sometimes she had to be force-fed; she'd acquired a hiatus hernia, gallstone trouble, a kidney infection. It was exhaustion, certainly, as well as an attack of Is-this-all-there-is? But there also still lingered the shock of the death of her father, and there had been some jarring ups and downs with the new man in her life, who lives in England—which was the only fact, incidentally, she'd reveal about him: though jovial and outspoken, Myles was protective of her personal life. She had to take stock, quiet down; and she did, a little.

"Before, it was just burn, burn, burn," she said during a pause in rehearsal in a cavernous hall in some desolate industrial area of L.A. "I was just relentless. I worked and I worked. No question I was successful. God, how can a human being who's so relentless not be?" We had just met. "Relentless" describes how in the next half-dozen hours she went at telling about herself, never veering off the topic; if briefly someone else was discussed it was strictly in connection to her; she wore self-interest like a safety helmet. Occasionally, she seemed to listen to herself and have trouble keeping a straight face (a tongue-in-cheek look she also sometimes gets singing). Was it a put-on? No, it wasn't that. She had on no make-up, no nail polish. She looked pale and a little drawn but her eyes were clear. She was dressed in a charcoal-grey woollen body stocking, a very long red gauze shirt, cowboy boots with silver toecaps, over the shirt her black leather jacket, and massive silver rings and chains and bangles ("Silver is the psychic alloy"). She designs all her "public" clothes, flying in a seamstress from Toronto: all part of the scrupulously tended image.

"Then came the dark time," Myles went on. "My body was collapsing and it affected my mind. I didn't understand why I was crying. There was this huge, terrible fear. It was loss of control—of myself. I thought I was going insane. And I went like: 'This is the wrong movie!' I felt very, very alone. I was pissed off with life. And this was a girl who had just accomplished all her dreams. It's been done now . . . I can die now. . . ."

Musicians wandered about the high-ceilinged hall stretching, lighting cigarettes, drinking from plastic bottles of distilled water. One with long blond hair, shirtless, a guitarist named Kurt Schefter from Toronto, ambled over and proffered Myles his bottle. No looks or words. He stared at her as she drank, his mind elsewhere. But he was right: she was thirsty.

"The lesson I learned was that I could stop trying so hard to prove myself. I learned that my fire was wearing me out—and hurting my loved one. Nobody can desire to be around someone who burns at all times. You exhaust that person. I exhaust myself. So I had to learn to find an inner peace, an equilibrium: to be positive. Now everything is coming to me. I hardly even have to work at the songs on the new album. The ideas and words come to me. Friends come to me. I'm the catalyst, the torch that fires up everyone around me." She giggled, "It's kinda neat."

"I never do anything half-assed. I throw myself into it. Sometimes that's painful. I feel a lot of the pains of the earth." Myles's concentration on what she was saying could at times become so fierce it was as if she was talking to herself. "Success is so surfacy but it's also deep. It has to do with why human beings exist in this world, and with loyalty, beliefs, hard work, and perseverance. I make music because it's important that I do and that the message is good. . . . I was pretty lost when I was young. . . . There were only male rock figures, who were evil, and there was the whole awful promiscuity thing. My heart goes out to those young girls looking up to me now. I've got to fucking give them a decent example!"

The musicians and the songwriter, Christopher Ward, Myles's boyfriend until four years ago and still it seemed her best male friend, had drifted back onto the scruffy stage. The long-legged singer joined them, moving in a swagger that only someone supremely at ease in her skin brings off. The ponytailed drummer, Jorn Anderson (also brought in from Toronto), ruffled a little bit of warm-up samba. And then they were fast and hard into the powerful "Our World, Our Times," a Ward song for the new album. There was high hope for it. As the producer, David Tyson (on keyboards; also from Toronto), affirmed: "This song will certainly never ever be a hit!"

The slight and rumpled Ward rocked gently on his heels, hands deep in his pockets, brown eyes always on Myles, on her mouth. Myles sang with her eyes often closed, her body quite still, in contrast to her usual performing persona—her strutting, stomping, bumping, grinding, high-kicking, head-swirling, bosom-shaking, snarling, grinning, slightly dangerous self. She sang in her bluesy, raspy, raunchy, hard-rock way that can rise to a shriek, then languidly dip low to grieve or yearn or caress; later she'd explain the importance of "what you don't sing." Minute hitches caused frequent stops and then Myles, Ward, and Tyson would confer quietly, amiably. Myles usually won. Once she really leaned into a passage and Tyson clutched his head: "I'll *pay* you, Alannah, if you do it my way." But no.

Myles is sensitive on the subject of control because she's been regarded as merely the creature of Svengalis Ward and Tyson, especially Ward. "If only people knew!" says Ward. "She drives the situation, not us. She owns the songs [I've written]. It's her desire and her will and her passion that binds people to the cause and motivates them." The two lived together in Toronto's Beaches district for eight years. Ward gained recognition as a writer/singer as well as a founding veejay of Canada's successful MuchMusic network. Myles worked at modelling, make-up, commercials, TV bit parts—anything to pay for taping demos for record-company executives to listen to and turn down. At that time, too, there occurred the "biggest hurt" in her life. When she moved in with Ward, her Catholic parents insisted she marry him; she refused, and was in effect ostracized for the next four years. She is the second oldest of five children; she told a family member in those days, "I know I'm eccentric, but I'm a good woman. There's a lot to love here." She says the anger, frustration, and pain in her singing came from then. Though she was reconciled with her father before he died, she stayed in her movie.

Manoeuvring her tan Mercedes sedan through the city's sluggish traffic, Myles decided to stop for iced tea by the pool at the Sunset Marquis (where she was dropping me off en route home). "I'm fuss-assed about quality," she said on the subject of control, to which she would return several times. "I know what I want. I'm a control freak. So everybody's learned just to bug out and let me make the decisions—about the music, the image. I also like the business end: I'm crafty. My dad taught me to try to bring out the best in people. It's nice to work in harmony and come home at night with a sore belly from laughing. The end result is art. The years of angst are behind me." Those years began at about nineteen, she said, when she loaded speakers and a guitar in the back of her car and drove around southern Ontario doing folk gigs in small-town coffee houses. Afterwards, alone, she wrote and sang songs and rehearsed her moves in front of motel-room mirrors. Christopher Ward recalls that on their first date Myles invited him back to her parents' place where she was living, took him downstairs, pulled out her guitar, and played him a song: "I knew where her passions were at from day one." Myles, however, remembered: "Like now, guys were always wanting to jump my bones." There were plenty of offers to help further her career.

The "years of angst" reminded her of the recent months on the road: "And here's Alannah and we dress her up (silk and silver, leather and lace), make her sing sexy: she's a product. And there's the reality of men chasing you down because you've become this sexual fantasy. That wasn't the message I wanted to project. I was disgusted. But I became hardened, blocked it out, tried to find solace.... That's probably another reason I got sick. I'm without my man, my family—there are no touchstones for me here. Life's between the studio, home, maybe dinner out, Christopher's place—that's about it."

"She's not a scene-maker at all," confirms Ward, who recently won a Song of the Year award for "Black Velvet" in L.A. from the American Society of Composers, Authors, and Publishers. "She just wants to accomplish something she can be proud of. In Canada I sense we're almost afraid of people who are confident to the point of being in your face. Alannah said, 'I'm going to make a hit. Get used to me.' She's no angel but I do love this person."

Myles circled the parking lot beneath the hotel. "I like earthy places. I'd like to live completely away from buildings, only go to buildings to work. I've rented a house overlooking the sea in an exquisite, wealthy neighbourhood. I picked it because I don't want to deal with riffraff. I'll be left alone, and I'll have neighbours who don't care about rock 'n' roll." The car came to a stop with a tiny screech.

Potted ficus and banana trees guarded the Sunset Marquis pool, around which were ranged white plastic lounge chairs with large coral-pink bath towels draped across their backs. It was late in the afternoon, but a few oiled, middle-aged men in sunglasses, with styled hair, still lay about conversing on cordless phones. Myles looked as if she felt at home. She ordered iced tea not with city water but Evian bottled water boiled first please. Then she whooped, leapt up, ran to a tall, moustached waiter moving like a dancer some tables away, and flung her arms around him, face against his chest. The hug had no reserve in it at all. Frank, she explained, swaggering back, every ageing shaded eye in step with her. "When I was ill here six months ago, he was there for me. He got me through the bad times. Sat with me. Didn't know who I was at first—and then he went out and bought my album and became a fan." From then, until Myles accepted my invitation to dinner and we moved inside, every time Frank passed near our table he was waved at and smiled at. Myles smiled more in that short while than she had in the previous three hours.

When Myles and two of her closest associates, Ward and his longtime friend and once fellow songwriter, Stephen Stohn, a Toronto entertainment lawyer, were individually asked what, in a word, was at the core of Myles's success, they gave the same answer. That's not surprising: the three have been friends for a decade. But I did wonder if "loyalty" was such a commonly cited ingredient for success in the music business. Or anywhere.

Stohn, whose clients include k.d. lang, Blue Rodeo, and Cowboy Junkies, insists that, along with loyalty, Myles's ability to focus also has to be mentioned. "You certainly get caught up in her maelstrom. She was a star long before the world recognized she was."

Ward says, flatly, "That's her story, loyalty. First she to me as a songwriter. Then I was loyal to her when the record companies kept turning us down. David Tyson worked with us for years for nothing. The loyalty goes down the line—musicians, sisters, sisters-in-law, friends, friends' sisters, and so on. It's such a tightly knit unit."

Myles ordered Manhattan clam chowder, a glass of milk, spicy-sauced pasta, fruit salad with whipped cream, and tea. From the food she might have eaten eight bites; she finished her milk and tea. "Food is just fuel," she apologized with a small smile. "But I'm enjoying this. It's very therapeutic to sit here and spill my guts out.

"When I needed it most, Christopher put his money where my mouth is." And "My confidence still sucks as a songwriter." And "Three years ago I would've begged to sing a commercial for $300. I've just turned down a jingle for $150,000, not because I can't use the money but because of what I owe my fans, and Christopher and David and everybody who've worked so hard to give me an image of class." And "I'd make a great mum, I'd love a kid." And "When I was young I was very self-centred, but I've never been a bad girl."

Dinner done, walking down to where she was parked, Myles said again how good the talking had felt. Minutes later she called on her car phone to say she'd pick me up tomorrow on her way to rehearsal.

Next morning she drove without speaking for a while. Then she said slowly: "I probably revealed far more yesterday than I feel comfortable about revealing." She hesitated. "I felt a little raped afterwards.

"I don't like revealing my private innermost thoughts. I've been very careful not to reveal any personality traits, past experiences—to anyone. So it's a natural feeling, I'm sure. Psychologically raped. Invaded."

Palm trees whizzed by. L.A.'s klieg-light sun beat down on the Mercedes that smelt of new leather.

It was all a little sad suddenly.

But as Myles wheeled the big car through the city's dusty streets, she recuperated, regained her form.

"Reading my story might change people's lives," she said after a bit. Then firmly: "I know from reading my mail that just making a record and presenting my image changed a lot of people's lives. Some were going to give up on their music until my record gave new hope. But they have to understand that you have to have extraordinary talent and willpower and tenacity and drive and desire in order to succeed. It's one in a million who makes it. I was one of those rare people."

Later, she revised her estimate upwards: one in *ten* million. Alannah knows no bounds.

24. The Tyrant's Touch (1990)

Last Thursday, Stuart Lockwood, aged five, stood straight and brave and calm for all the world to see. Dressed in blue soccer shorts and a white shirt, arms crossed firmly in front of his chest, the English boy seemed to be staring past the burly man in the business suit sitting in a chair next to him. Maybe he was looking at his mother, who was among the 26 or so other hostages and the military officers in the room where the cameras were working.

The man talked to Stuart and as he was talking his big left hand for a moment gently took hold of the boy's right arm by the elbow, then stroked his hair. Stuart stood, his face quiet, and let Saddam Hussein, president of Iraq, talk to him and touch him. A man sitting off to the side repeated the president's words in English so Stuart and all the rest of us would understand them. Stuart couldn't have known what sort of being Saddam Hussein was, only that he was dangerous.

In the next few days the picture of Stuart standing there so alone would enter our minds many times from television and from newspapers. What was said is fading, but Stuart stays—like the young man halting the column of tanks in Beijing's Tiananmen Square in June last year, like John-John Kennedy saluting his father's coffin, like other such pictures; we each have our own.

Stuart didn't jerk his arm or his head away when Saddam Hussein put his hand there; he didn't move even a little. His small body said clearly it didn't want to be touched but Stuart let it be touched. You could see he was tense, but not if he was afraid, which he must have been. How did he know to stay so calm? I think it was a woman who told him, probably his mother, or an older sister or an aunt or a neighbour, but almost certainly a woman. In the days and hours before those cameras were set up and the bright lights turned on in that room somewhere in Iraq, I think that woman talked to Stuart quietly, with no panic in her voice, about the mad and deadly world they had suddenly landed in and that she wanted them to come out of alive.

That "mad world" was just here for a while, she would have said, and promised the world Stuart knew would come back again. One day everybody would be happy once more. But now, she had to talk to him about things to do with right now; and if she repeated herself he should be patient because she wanted him to clearly understand what she said and to remember it.

I may be wrong, but I think women are often better than men at teaching the calmness, courage and common sense it takes to live through brutal times, especially to children. Is it that women at such times are able to think more about the person they're trying to reach than about themselves? Are they able to give their words such exactness, fit them so perfectly, that the words become the other person's own?

When I was about seven, a bit older than Stuart, I began a three-and-half-year stay in Japanese prison camps. I lived in what is now Indonesia, on the island of Java, in the city of Bandung, in a small house my mother, my older brother, Jerry, and I shared with three other Dutch families. Around one part of the city they had built a high bamboo fence topped with barbed wire and 5,000 of us lived inside the fence. The camp was guarded by soldiers with rifles with bayonets on the end and they would only let you out if you were extremely sick (that was in the early days) or dead. The place was called *Bloemenkamp*, which means "Camp of Flowers," and it held women, girls and small boys. Men and older boys were in other prisons far away; my father was in one of those, and in about a year, when Jerry turned 12, he would be trucked to one also.

The three of us lived in what used to be a storage room, with one mattress for my mother and one for Jerry and me, and a wooden box that was our table. During the day my mother and Jerry worked for the soldiers, in the vegetable gardens, the kitchen, the above-ground sewers; I was still too young to work and, as there was no school, I played all day.

In the evening the three of us would sit around the box, on which burned a smoky oil lamp. We would talk in low voices for only a little while because the days were hot and long and my mother and Jerry needed their sleep. We would talk about what happened that day and about "the old days" when we had lots of eggs and fruit salad. We could see each other's eyes shine. Jerry and I did most of the talking and my mother listened. She was very good at that and still is. Sometimes, though, she would insist on speaking and often she was serious then. You could tell because her lips grew thin.

I remember one such time among many: I had told a story of an adventure I'd had that day with a well-known guard called Jantje Tomaat (Johnny Tomato). He had this name because, as he patrolled the camp on his bicycle, he would keep an eye out for edible tomatoes in the little vegetable plots prisoners were still permitted. If he spotted a red one, he'd jump off his bike, pluck it and eat it on the spot. It was foolish to let your tomatoes ripen on the plant. That day he picked a tomato in the front yard of the people across the street. He saw me looking at him eating it, and I quickly straightened my shoulders and bowed from the waist as was the rule.

Jantje Tomaat grinned at me and swung onto his bike—it was known that he liked little kids. I watched him slowly ride down our street and then, just before he reached the corner, there was a woman who either hadn't bowed quickly or deeply enough, or maybe he didn't like her face. Anyway, Jantje Tomaat got off his bike and holding the steering wheel in the middle with his left hand walked yelling up to the woman who was still bowed forward and rammed the front wheel between her legs and hit her with the flat of his right hand many times on the sides of her head, on her ears, until she crumpled onto the road. Then he climbed back on his bike and pedalled around the corner.

I ran over to where the woman lay. Two women who'd also seen what happened were carefully helping her sit up. Her head was wobbling, her eyes stared, not even crying.

My mother had listened and then, lips thin, she spoke slowly, as she had done before and would again: "They are your enemy. Always remember that. They have guns and they are dangerous. They don't like you, even if they smile at you. They don't like any of us. We are their enemy and if we disobey them or get in their way they will kill us. Always be polite, always be serious, always stay calm. Don't laugh, don't smile, don't joke. You may lie if something in you tells you that you must. I am afraid and I know that you are afraid. But you'll be less afraid if you remember what I'm telling you."

We don't know what the words were that helped Stuart Lockwood stand so brave those few moments in his life, but at the heart of danger clearly the right words spoke to him.

25. My Wound (1989)

I got my wound when I was seven. I was living on the Indonesian island of Java, in the city of Bandung, in a small house my mother, my older brother Jerry, and I shared with three other families. There was a war going on, and the enemy had won. Around one part of the city they had built a high bamboo fence topped with barbed wire. The fence had one gate and it was guarded day and night by soldiers with rifles with bayonets on the end. We lived inside the fence with about five thousand other people. It was a prison. The only reason soldiers would let you through the gate was if you were extremely sick or dead.

The place was called *Bloemenkamp*, which means "Camp of Flowers," and it held women, girls, and small boys. Men and older boys were in other prisons far away. My father was in one of those and in about a year, when Jerry turned twelve, he would be taken to one also.

In *Bloemenkamp* I never wore a shirt or socks or shoes, only shorts, because the weather was so hot and because there was no school. If you were little you stayed at home and played all day. If you were bigger, or if you were a grownup, the soldiers made you work for them—in the kitchens, gardens, and above-ground sewers. So I was alone a lot because my mother and Jerry had to work. Another thing: there was never enough to eat. When you're hungry, you can't talk or think or even dream about anything else but food. Worse, your body grows weak. And then, if you get sick, you don't have the strength to fight back and you become sicker. There was no medicine in *Bloemenkamp*. The only people who knew anything about sickness were two nurses with grey hair who laughed a lot and lived in a garage.

In our house there were four mothers, twelve children, and one toilet. You often had to wait in line to go. If I only had to pee, nobody minded if I went in the back of the garden among some banana trees. The garden was divided in four pieces where each family grew vegetables for extra food. A part of our piece of garden, about as big as a dining-room table, my mother left empty for me to play in. The earth was often wet from rain and I liked to build castles, forts, the decks of ships, and to dig secret tunnels.

One day, lying on my stomach working on a tunnel, I brought out my right hand full of earth and saw a little bit of blood on the middle knuckle of my forefinger. It didn't hurt. Maybe there was a sliver of glass in the ground. I wiped the finger on my pants, but more blood seeped out. So I went to the kitchen and held my finger under the water tap and when the water washed away the earth I could see a cut as tiny as an eyelash. The bleeding soon stopped, and I went back to digging my tunnel.

That evening the knuckle was red and the edges of the cut swollen. My mother cleaned the cut and wrapped a strip of bedsheet around it.

Next morning, the whole finger was red and swollen. It hurt, and it hurt more and more as that day went by, and in the middle of the night that followed the pain woke me up. The finger was now twice as thick as the others. The cut had turned yellow. My body was warm. My mother made a pan of hot water with salt in it and set the pan on the wooden box that was our table. Jerry woke up and came and sat with me on the edge of our mattress and put his arms around me. My mother slowly put my hand in the pan and told me to leave it there. She said the hot salt water would soak the yellow dirt out of the cut. It was the dirt that was causing the pain.

"It's not a cut anymore," she said, "it's a wound."

Next to the pan on the box burned our oil lamp that smoked. My mother sat on her mattress and the three of us talked in whispers so we wouldn't wake up the other families. We each had a spoonful of sugar from our tin. The water cooled off and she heated more. The skin of my hand got soft but the wound stayed closed.

In the morning, before she went to work, my mother took me to see the two nurses in their garage. They laughed and gave me a piece of cold pancake but said that what I needed was lot of food and vitamins. This was their last pancake, though, and they certainly didn't have any vitamins. My mother went to work and I went home and lay on her mattress and listened to insects in the hot air. I didn't move, but I was wet with sweat. It was as if a clock were ticking inside my finger. There was yellow all over my hand and even my wrist was swollen and red. If I moved my arm even a little, it hurt. When my mother and Jerry came home from work there was a thin red line running from the finger across my hand and up my arm to the elbow. My mother looked at me and said, "That's blood poisoning." Her lips grew thin. "We have to do something," she said. She looked at Jerry. "Watch him," she said, nodding at me, and then she went out.

Her lips were still thin when she came back later. She said she had talked to the nurses again. Drawing on me with her finger, she explained that the red line might run higher and higher up my arm, and then across my chest right to my heart. That was dangerous, the nurses had told her. Before that happened, they had said, they would have to put me on a table and cut off my hand or even a part of my arm!

"Well," said my mother, and she took my chin in her hand and looked at me, "we don't want that. So you're going on a trip—tomorrow."

* * * * *

Early the next morning she and I walked to a house near the prison gate. My mother knocked. A girl opened the door and inside there was a very old woman sitting in a wheelchair with a blue blanket spread over her legs. "You're going to sit there on that little step," said my mother. "We're going to pull the blanket down over you. Then we're going to wheel you down the street and through the gate. Somebody will lift this lady and you in a truck. The truck is going to a hospital where there's food and vitamins." The girl and the old woman were looking at me but didn't say anything.

"Stay under the blanket and be very quiet," my mother said. "If the soldiers at the gate catch you they won't let you or the lady out. Do you understand?" Then she took my face between her hands and kissed me long on one cheek and then on the other.

"Remember," she said, "it's an adventure."

I climbed between the old woman's legs, the blanket came down, and the wheelchair began to move. It bumped out of the door and the bumps shot into my arm. It was hot under the blanket, and I could smell the old woman. We rolled along and nobody said a word. We stopped and men's voices started yelling.

There was a clank and a squeaking and then the chair rolled on again and then it stopped. I felt us swing through the air and then thump down, almost falling over—in the back of the truck, I guessed.

This was long ago. I remember that when we got to the hospital the old woman in her chair wheeled herself down a hall and I didn't see her again. A nurse in a long white dress that whispered and a stiff cap that hid her hair took me to a room full of beds with children in them and gave me a cup of fruit salad. She wore a black cross on a silver chain around her neck.

I remember that I was the healthiest child in that room, and the only one allowed to walk around. The others were also younger than I, except for a boy I discovered in a little room by himself. His name was Peter and he had a white face, hair so blond it was almost white, and huge blue eyes. He told me right away that his left leg had been caught under the wheel of a horse-drawn moving van. He smelled terrible.

Under his bedsheet his leg lay inside a wire cage, specially built for it, he told me, but he never let me see it.

Peter was a favourite of the nurses. Every day they went into his room to say hello. They were busy, but they always had time for him. When they came running by, I would ask, "How's Peter?" and then I'd get a smile.

You would think Peter liked all the attention, but he didn't. He told me he had heard the nurse talking about his leg when they thought he was asleep. He had already had three operations, but soon, he was sure, it would be all over and he would go home. And even if they did cut off his leg, he said, it didn't matter. One day he would be a soldier—like his father, who was dead—and he knew for sure you could be a soldier just as well on one leg. He would then talk about weapons and marching. He knew a lot and he never laughed. What I didn't like was that he did all the talking and was always so sure about everything. When I showed him my yellow hand on the first day he hardly looked at it. His leg was much worse, he said. All I needed was food and vitamins.

Of that time I remember listening to Peter, eating a lot, swallowing vitamins, and watching the nurses run by in their whispering dresses. Several times a day I had to sit at a desk in a little room with glass walls, in the middle of the big room, from where you could see all the beds, and hold my hand in a bowl of hot water and salt to soak out the dirt. A nurse would take me in and not come back until the water was cold. It hurt so much I had to cry. Everybody, of course, could see me through the glass walls, so what I did then was sing as loud as I could with my hand in the water so that nobody would think I was crying. Over and over again, I sang:

My bonnie lies over the ocean,
My bonnie lies over the sea,
My bonnie lies over the ocean,
Oh bring back my bonnie to me.

There are many words to this song, but I sang what I knew.

It took seventeen days in the hospital for my wound to heal. In the late afternoon of the last day the nurses put me in the back of a truck full of mothers and children going to the prison for the first time. When we got to the gate it had grown almost dark. The soldiers on guard just didn't notice the extra boy. My mother and brother had come to the gate every evening, which was when new people came in and they were waiting. My mother kissed me long on both cheeks and laughed and said, "Thank God for small mercies," and Jerry put his arm around me. I showed them my finger right away. It's the same as the other fingers, except the skin over the knuckle isn't rumpled but smooth, and shows a tiny pink line no bigger than an eyelash.

26. Hubie and I (1990)

Hubie van Boxel became my best friend, but I did have to get used to him. He and his mother and two grown-up sisters moved into our barrack some months after my mother and I were already settled in. She and I had been transported from camp to camp for more than three years and had lost many friends. This camp, Kampong Makasar, was our last: the war would end in a few weeks—but we didn't know that. We were on the Indonesian island of Java near the city of Batavia (Jakarta now) in July, 1945. Makasar held about 3,500 women and children (men and older boys lived in separate camps, we didn't know where); most of us were Dutch, and we were prisoners of the Japanese government.

I watched Hubie and the three women put away clothes, bedding, tin mugs, eating pans. The women's eyes seemed always to be on him. I would learn later that anything he asked for they would give him, if they had it, or bring to him, like a drink of water. He looked about my age, nearly eleven, and my size, which made him the other biggest boy in the camp. His mother strung up a pair of riding boots from a rafter above their sleeping space on the bamboo bed that stretched the barrack's length. On the bed opposite, near the front entrance, my mother and I had 60 plus 50 centimetres of space. In between the beds ran a path of red earth.

It wasn't just Hubie's family who treated him as if he were special—everybody did. He smiled a lot, which wasn't usual, and he was polite, which many children weren't any more. But I thought the interest in him was probably because of his hair, which grew in tiny curls tight against his head and was golden. That's the word people used, golden. And because his mother and sisters looked after him so well, so that in the heat he always looked fresh and clean, there was a shine to it. Anyhow, people seemed to enjoy seeing Hubie, even the guards, I think. I heard some women and girls and even my mother say about Hubie: "He looks like an angel."

Still, in that place, as the two biggest boys (all boys twelve and older, like my brother, Jerry, had by then been taken to other camps because they were a danger to the state), we had to become friends. We would otherwise have had to fight until it became clear which one of us won most often. I learned not to mind that people's eyes always followed Hubie.

There was no school but, like everybody over nine, we worked. For us this meant the vegetable gardens outside the camp's high bamboo fence. We hacked at the ground, weeded, carried water, as the sky turned white in the heat of the sun. In the middle of the gardens stood a shed where in hot, still air six pigs were growing fat for the officers. Boys and young girls wore only shorts, so that even if we had had a chance to steal vegetables we had no place to hide them; and neither, really, did the older girls and women who wore blouses, or brassieres, or tea towels tied across their chests. Dust from the red earth mixed with sweat and dried into crusts. But most days after work we were permitted to use the bath huts—dark, slippery places that held oil drums brimming with water. You dipped a can in and splashed yourself. People laughed there and yelped. The water falling from arms stretched high made bodies glisten.

Around that time my mother said that I was becoming a big boy and should bathe separately. Hubie's mother told him the same thing. The two women had not talked about this. Hubie's mother worked in the camp office, mine in the gardens; his father was a high-up army officer, mine had had a job on a tea plantation. Mrs. Van Boxel held her head high and seldom spoke to anyone. We obeyed our mothers and bathed by ourselves. Sometimes, while waiting, we'd go to a hole in the back of the bath hut and stare.

There was a sameness to time in Makasar. After bathing, Hubie and I roamed the camp, circling barracks, the office, the hospital, the kitchen, checking the high fence for holes. A hole meant someone had tried to smuggle in food, oranges or bananas for a scarf or a wedding ring. But few had anything left to barter with and it was dangerous.

Our commandant was a small, thin man, whose mouth was formed as if he were smiling. He and his officers lived in a stone house just outside the camp's main gate. No matter how hot it was, he always wore a starched military jacket, wide pants for horseback riding, and polished riding boots. The few times a woman was caught smuggling food, always at night, the guard would run her over to the stone house, up the steps onto the veranda. There her hair would be cut off with barber's clippers, some of it getting ripped out roots and all. Then the commandant would yell at her and hit and kick her until he grew tired. Our barrack, 4A, was near the gate, and we could hear what happened. Afterwards the woman was locked in a cage for a few days with only a little water.

Women took these risks because they were hungry. That's also why Hubie and I wandered around after bathing: we were looking for food. Sometimes we would sneak away long after the lights had gone out at eight and it was forbidden to be outside. We did this even though we knew that, while we might get a few slaps if caught, our mothers would be really punished. We'd meet at the latrine, a long gully over which you squatted, then run from shadow to shadow through the empty camp to the kitchen. There might be some burnt rice at the bottom of a cooking pot, or a swallow of soup. A food shed might have been left unlocked. One of these held hard, brick-sized cakes of pig food called *bungkil.* It was softened in water for the pigs, and people could eat it like that or roasted. A blue line sometimes ran through a cake, and this was said to be poisonous to humans. Once or twice we had found a hunk of *bungkil*; it tasted a little like sand.

On our last night run, Hubie and I found nothing in the pots and the sheds were locked—but then we spotted a hole near the ground in the wall of the *bungkil* shed. Hubie reached in and brought out almost half a cake. We broke it into pieces and roasted them in the still-hot ashes of a kitchen fireplace, then climbed onto the kitchen's palm-leaf roof and sat very still, close together, nibbling the *bungkil.* We felt it filling us. We felt strong and we wanted to laugh and punch each other. We ate it all—there was no thought of sharing. In a little while we slid down, ran back, and lay down beside our sleeping mothers.

Two or three hours later that same night beating sounds and screams started coming from the stone house. They went on and on, until just before six, when, as every day, a bell called us to stand in front of the barracks to be counted. In rows of five, we'd bow deeply as the soldiers walked by, those in front counting loud and very fast in Japanese.

That morning the commandant himself came by. Beside him walked the translator and behind him, wearing only panties and brassieres, followed two young women, each held up by a soldier; they were bald now and covered in black bruises and blood. The commandant spoke, seeming to smile, and the translator told us that he had decided that no prisoner must ever again try to smuggle in food of which he gave us plenty. He had punished the women, as we could see, and now he would punish the whole camp: we must remain inside our barrack for the next two days and we would not be fed. Then the little group moved on to the next barrack.

No-one now felt sorry for the two young women. We brought in water in our mugs and eating pans, we talked softly, dozed. My mother said we should stay this quiet to save our strength; we had no reserves of food. Because of the two hunger days people got sick, and patients in the hospital and some older women died.

On the third day, Hubie didn't show up in the gardens. Someone said she'd seen him being carried to the hospital. I went there after bathing, but the nurse wouldn't let me in. Mrs. van Boxel and her daughters in the meantime had hung sheets like curtains around their bed space. The next day we heard something that was hard to believe: the Japanese were taking Hubie to the military hospital in Batavia.

Along with his crying mother and sisters, at least a dozen people were waiting at the camp gate early next morning when Hubie was carried through on a stretcher and lifted into the back of a truck. He lay curled up, not seeing us, looking about half my size.

Mrs. van Boxel stayed behind her sheets. Some days went by and then my mother took me for a little walk. She said she had heard that the military doctors had done their very best for Hubie. They had all liked him, she said; anything he wanted they had given him. Apparently he had asked for sliced bananas with milk and brown sugar.

I stood outside Mrs. van Boxel's sleeping space that night and listened to the crying. I stayed awake, and when it was late I saw someone slip from behind the sheets. It was Mrs. van Boxel wrapped in a big towel with a smaller one over her head. I got up and followed. At the latrine I sat down a distance behind her; there must have been stars because I could see the white skin of her back. I whispered that I was sorry that Hubie was dead. The head under the towel turned a little and nodded. I asked if she knew we had eaten from the same piece of *bungkil*. She nodded again. Then I heard her whisper that she didn't want to face her husband because, oh, he would be so sad about losing his son.

Time in Makasar speeded up. There were rumours the war was ending—really, this time. And yes, there I was one day sitting on the bamboo fence, yelling and waving at an airplane dropping parachutes beneath which swung big wooden boxes. The boxes held canned food, chocolate, medicine, and cigarettes. From somewhere there appeared a gramophone and jazz records and that night, in another barrack, women with cigarettes between their lips danced together until very late. I danced too and they gave me puffs.

Suddenly there were English soldiers in the stone house and a truck drove off with our guards packed in the back. The big gate was left standing open. My father walked through it one afternoon, looking smaller; he kept touching my mother and me, not letting go of our hands. He said we were a lucky family because my brother, Jerry, had landed in the same camp as he in a town. We were now going to that camp by train to live in a real house.

One of Hubie's sisters came over before we left to say her mother wanted me to have some of his things: a soft wool cap such as Frenchmen wear, a plaster soldier on a horse, and the riding boots that had hung from the rafter. She said her mother had kept the boots all these years so Hubie could wear them to run to his father when he saw him again.

Jerry was waiting for us, taller, more serious; still, it hardly seemed to matter there were four years between us. He and I liked to climb to the ridge of the roof of the house and straddle it. One day we were fighter pilots, arms stretched sideways, weaving and diving, strafing enemy soldiers running below. We had turned and were swooping back—when I put my arms down and started to cry. Jerry flew on a moment, looked back, then climbed around me and off the roof. It was real crying, sobbing and coughing—Hubie was so alive in my mind I kept saying his name. After a while he began to fade and I went on with the day.

It happened again, during a meal, and I left the table and sat down on the floor in another room facing the wall. My family let me be. I thought of Hubie certainly as I cried, and of others.

And one last time—at the start of an evening in the camp that wasn't one any more, when a violinist from Hungary stood on a chair in a field and played for hundreds of men and women and children sitting around him on the ground. I put my head down when the thought of Hubie came along, but then I looked up and saw that playing the violin was such hard work that the man's face was actually shining with sweat.

27. Back on Java (1990)

I sat near the edge of the pond and watched for fish jumping; I never saw any, only the widening rings they left behind. The ample pond was stocked with carp and gourami. Monsoon rains had raised the brown water almost level with the lush lawn and shrubs. My wrought-iron chair stood beside the front door of a two-room guest-house overgrown by an orange bougainvillea. It was light but the sun didn't show yet; ordinary birds had taken over from the noisy creatures of the night. This was the best time. Once the sun appeared the heat would soon follow—heat that you breathed and tasted and could see dancing in the hazy air.

There was time; by now a routine had evolved. Renni wouldn't come over from the main house with the tray of tea and sliced papaya for another half-hour. I had been awake for hours already: tropical nightlife was still disconcerting. In the dark, inside my little house and around it, there was much rustling, whirring, and the odd squeal, and around 4:30 the muezzins' voices calling the faithful to prayer would swell to a great wail.

During most of a short stay in Indonesia last winter, I moved along in a kind of dream state—every sight and sound and smell set off waves of memories. Back in Canada I had made no specific plans. I wasn't a tourist. This morning I would be leaving the city of Bogor on a small journey that would take me about 100 kilometres south into the mountains in search of a tea plantation, difficult of access. My father, a Dutchman, had been one of the administrators there before the Second World War. I had lived on the island of Java from three to the age of fourteen. For me, remembered consciousness began there. In a sense I was going home.

Somewhere back in the garden a woman began to sing tonelessly, on and on. I watched big red ants marching along a branch of bougainvillea up to the roof, one behind the other. It would be good to get away from Bogor's closeness. To escape the swampy coastal heat you have to travel at least 20 kilometres further south. Yet Bogor is cooler than Jakarta, the capital, 60 kilometres to the north. Jakarta, with a population of around 11 million, is just bearable at night; to survive during the day takes immense stamina and patience.

A week earlier I'd landed there, as most visitors to the country do. The city is a magnet for Indonesians, the nerve centre of their remarkable—and little-known—country. Indonesia comprises 13,677 islands, which, when imposed on a map of the United States, stretch from Oregon to Bermuda. Its 180 million citizens from 300 ethnic groups speak 250 languages and form the world's fifth most populous country. One hundred and ten million Indonesians live on the island of Java, which is only as big as England—and every year uncounted thousands of them drift into Jakarta. The city boasts luxury hotels, handsome boulevards, fine museums, a number of office towers, twelve daily newspapers, and Southeast Asia's largest mosque. About 80 per cent of foreign investment stops in Jakarta first; the deals are made there and the rake-offs dispensed. But what the newcomers are more likely to encounter are endless expanses of slums—easily the equal of those of Calcutta or Dhaka or Lagos—garbage-choked waterways, snarled traffic, thousands of starving, diseased, and crazed individuals roaming the streets, and a sewage and drainage system so outdated that, when the rains come, two-thirds of Jakarta is flooded. And there's the heat.

We had lived in Jakarta for a few years after the war, my parents, my brother, Jerry, and I. There was much unrest in the streets: fighting had started almost immediately after the Japanese occupation forces capitulated to the Allies in 1945. The Indonesians wanted independence, but the Dutch, who had dominated the islands for 350 years, said no. "Police actions" and "pacification exercises" were launched and bloodily pursued until the Indonesians, cheered on by world opinion, finally managed to toss the Dutch out in 1949.

Our family had already returned to Holland by then: my brother and I needed proper schooling. The war years had been spent in Japanese prison camps and before that on the isolated plantation. In Jakarta, between shootouts and rabies scares, schools closed almost every other day. By leaving in 1948, we missed the independence celebrations put on by the new republic's flamboyant President Sukarno, with the crowds screaming *Merdeka!* (Freedom!) in the heart of his capital, a one-square-kilometre neglected park—right across the street from our house.

A sleek high-rise had replaced our home, and government buildings, banks, and hotels now crowded the square. In the middle of it rose the 130-metre National Monument, a marble obelisk with thirty-five kilos of pure gold gilding its crowning flame, built to commemorate the struggle for freedom. I remembered the empty field where goats had grazed. Once it had held mystery for me. Where the obelisk now stood there had been a dry and rusted fountain. By day I had dared approach it with a friend. By night yells and wild laughter could be heard, but I never got close enough even to distinguish men from women in the light of their little fires. On our day excursions we saw only women, as many as 20, their faces white with make-up powder, young, middle-aged, some nursing babies, cooking, washing, picking at each other's heads, sleeping in the shade of lean-tos made of trash. They wore their blouses unbuttoned, or no blouses, and their long oily hair hung loose. Their arms and shoulders were burned nearly black, like those of beggars. They would screech and flap their small hands for us to come closer and take teasing little runs at us; they moved so it looked at first as if they were gently dancing. Cackling, they would make gestures with those small hands that we understood at once. We laughed with them and then turned and trotted home, feeling older.

On the way out of Jakarta's furor, I had asked the English-speaking driver, Rusli Sunanjaya, if we could find out whether anything was left of the last prison camp I'd been in at age ten. Located outside Jakarta, on a small road to Bogor, Kampung Makasar, one of many on Java, had held about 3,500 mostly Dutch women and children. Rusli and I discovered that the village of the same name that had been near the camp had grown into an entire city district. Clerks at the municipal offices had never heard of a camp, but then none of them looked over forty. They wanted to help, though, and were able to guide us to the house of Hajji Mohamad Nur, a retired fruit farmer, who had been a village official in the 1940s.

Tall, straight, 75 years old, and a chain smoker of Indonesia's clove-spiced cigarettes, Nur waved his big hands around and was inclined to shout though he wasn't deaf. It was a pleasure, he said, to have us in his house, though unexpected. He was called Hajji, I should understand, because he had made the pilgrimage to Mecca. The camp, he said, had been a "bad and secret" place—bamboo barracks surrounded by a high fence in the middle of vegetable gardens. White women and children worked there. Nur thought his wife, his blind, 90-year-old mother-in-law, and he himself were probably the only ones left who remembered. About three-quarters of the people in the area had died in those years, first when the enemy army took away the food the farmers grew and afterwards during the revolution. He pointed at my driver, at me, and then at himself, clapped his hands, and laughed loudly: "We have all survived!"

I didn't know what to say.

And neither did he then, I think, so he showed us around his small stone house. Oil-lamp smoke had blackened the ceiling of the front room. In a second, even dimmer room hung an oil portrait of Nur in the 1940s, as tall and straight as now.

I asked if anyone had ever felt *kasihan* for those whites? The exact word for pity had leapt to mind. "Of course!" he said. Young men from the village would make their way to the camp after midnight with fruit or other food, to exchange for clothes or jewellery. But sometimes they'd feel such *kasihan* they'd just throw the food over the fence and run home. He shrugged.

After the women and children had been evacuated from Makasar, the Allies filled the filthy barracks with Japanese prisoners. Today it is an army garrison built of stone, but there's still, as then, a lot of barbed wire about. We drove by later, en route to Bogor. The road is wider and busier, but the main gate, through which as a child I'd peered at freedom, is just where it used to be. According to Nur, neighbourhood people are superstitious about it: since 1945, accidents in which someone is always killed have been happening in front of the gate. "Many people died inside that place," Nur explained, "and their spirits are still there!"

Once in Bogor, whether by luck or by the connivance of the ever-present "silent forces"—it's easy to accept the mysteries of the spirit world there—my lack of planning began to prove providential. An acquaintance in Canada had asked me to drop off a couple of paperbacks at the home of a zoologist friend, Kathy MacKinnon. She promptly used her credentials to arrange a room in the boarding house for scientists visiting the world-famous Bogor Botanical Gardens. It was late when we drove into the deserted grounds of Kebon Raya, the 87-hectare park and research centre. Stopping by a tall house looming in the dark, she directed me to walk ahead to a small light aswarm with insects. The motor's sound faded quickly in the high-pitched thrumming from the trees and bushes beyond the road. The air was hot and moist and overhead things whooshed by, receding fast, coming back. In addition to the flora, the gardens were host to a colony of bats with huge wingspans and bodies the size of rats. Don't run, I thought.

Out of the blackness at that moment came a thin bent old man, wrapped in a sarong, barefoot, smiling, folded hands out in greeting: I was safe. On the plantation there had been men like that staying up all night, cigarettes gleaming in the dark, guarding us whites, our homes, our trucks, the tea factory. Old men usually, but they kept away the evils of the night. When it stormed and the souls of children wept in the trees, it was good to know they were out there, smoking, watching.

The next morning, when I delivered another package from the same Canadian acquaintance, I met Renni Samsoedin. Renni has degrees in botany and chemistry and works in research in a building ten minutes' walk from Kebon Raya's main gate. The gardens are in the middle of Bogor; the city has grown up around them. An attractive, immensely cheerful woman in her early thirties, Renni spoke fluent English and asked why I was in Indonesia. I told my story of wanting to see the place where I'd lived as a boy. She nodded and smiled and nodded. When you talk to Indonesians, it seems sometimes that part of their consciousness is elsewhere, as if they are dreaming and yet awake.

"Ah well," Renni said suddenly, "we must make a plan. You must come and stay where I live—there's lots of room. Of course, you will want to meet my father. He will help with the plan."

Renni was intrigued by the idea of someone returning to where he'd been small—and in *her* Indonesia. It would not do to muddle on alone, though. Just rent a car and go? It wasn't that simple. Or maybe it was, but it was no fun. Or at least it was more fun if Indonesians came along to explain things. Her whole family would help make a plan. There were three girls and seven boys, all adults; Cucu, the youngest, was 22. What's more, her father had been Kebon Raya's chief administrator until he retired in 1978, and their house had been right on the grounds. That her family and I should now meet was, well, "magical."

Would I return to her office at the end of the day when Cucu picked her up in the Land Rover—and would I like *saté ayam* (chicken roasted on bamboo skewers in spicy peanut sauce) with *nasi goreng* (fried rice) for supper?

Much of that day I roamed through Kebon Raya, with its rolling lawns, holy banyan trees, cactus gardens, lily ponds, and forest groves. Opened in 1817 by the Dutch, the park contains 15,000 species of tropical plants and trees (including 400 types of palms) and the nurseries house more than 4,500 orchid varieties. It was green and still. Upside down from the branches of a dead-looking tree hung the bats from the night before. Now and then one would wake up with a cry of grief, spread its cloaklike wings, float to another branch, and fold up again. The massive, many-trunked holy trees possessed immense self-assurance: roots grew down from their branches into the earth, enlarging and renewing them forever. It was safe in their shadow.

Beyond the gardens' main gate the street was noisy, busy, the air grey with exhaust fumes. Returning to Renni's office, I followed the narrow, crowded sidewalk that hugged Kebon Raya's fence of iron bars. I spotted the figure from 30 metres away. She squatted motionless with her back to the traffic, her head tucked face-down between her knees, her arms around her shins nearly touching the fence. She was a small, not-old woman, stark naked, pressed together as once in the womb, her skin streaked with dirt, crusts of it in her hair. She was in no-one's way and no-one paid attention. Her turned-away body begged to die. Despair speaks out everywhere, but sometimes there's a long echo.

Later at Renni's house the rest of the family wasn't home yet. She first showed me, spread out on the floor, polished and ready, enough flutes, bamboo xylophones, gongs, and other percussion instruments for an entire *gamelan* ensemble. On Sundays the Samsoedins get together and perform Indonesia's rhythmically complex, liquid, thousand-year-old music for hours on end; but I missed that. Renni walked me around the family's terraced fairy-tale garden, full of still places, to the little guesthouse by the fish pond where I would sleep.

Most of the family came around that evening. Word got out about Renni's foreigner, though none of them has a phone. All knew some English. Pak Samsoedin, the father, also remembered a few words of Dutch. Soft-spoken and much less direct than his daughter, he did eventually ask why I was in Indonesia. Halfway through my reply his attention shifted in that curious Indonesian way.

"So," he said abruptly in English-Dutch, dropping in a word of French as well, "you are going on a journey of *nostalgie*?" He stared ahead. The room was quiet. "I too would like to go on a journey of *nostalgie*. And in the same area. It is beautiful. High in the mountains with the tea. . . . I was stationed there, you know—in 1947, with the army."

That would have been the revolutionary army fighting the Dutch.

"I remember we were put up in a nice house," he went on. "In the morning I would go out and do my exercises on the big flat lawn. . . ."

He paused, remembering.

I thought I felt some neck hairs rise. I reached for my camera bag and felt inside for a half dozen tiny black-and-white pictures taken before the war.

"And then I would walk to the edge of the lawn," he resumed, "and look down at my friends playing soccer on the field below. . . ."

I held out a photo.

"This house?"

He looked.

"That house, yes."

It was a picture of *our* first house on the plantation. We'd been trucked away in 1942. The population of Java is *110 million* . . . and *forty-seven* years later . . . ! The family was amused but not awestruck: these things happen. Renni laughed and said, "Magic!" Her father took it entirely in stride and continued to reminisce about his army days. But yes, the journey of *nostalgie*. . . .

Cucu should drive me. Cucu was on a break from law school and had time. In a corner on the floor with his seven-year-old niece Dini in his lap, Cucu nodded sleepily. Short and slight, he rarely spoke and always looked sleepy—

but he handled the powerful Land Rover as if it were a toy. Pak Samsoedin thought his son would probably want along as navigator his best friend, Yadi, also a student of law, and free. Cucu nodded. Renni said that if I could wait a couple of days, she'd take time off and come as interpreter. Absolutely. Other Samsoedins suggested they'd like to go. By all means. The map was spread out on the floor, the jug of chilled coconut juice did the rounds, a route was plotted. The "silent forces" were at it all right. There was a great honking of frogs in the fish pond.

The road started to ascend on leaving Bogor and the air grew drier and cooler. Every day since I'd arrived in Indonesia there had been the season's sudden rain squalls, but today it stayed dry and mostly sunny, allowing the views along the twisting, climbing roads to come spectacularly into their own. Early on, patches of mist had raced over the valleys, over the tender green, terraced rice fields. Where the hillsides carried cuts or stood too steep there was unruly jungle growth from which poked the familiar heads of coconut trees. Later, high up where the tea plantings began, the terrain acquired the long sweep of mid-ocean waves: the flat-topped, black-green bushes fell and rose in patterned clusters against the red earth from the shadows of one mountain into those of the next. Renni (only she, Cucu, and Yadi had finally been able to come along) called the weather "magic," as she labelled almost everything slightly fortuitous. But she was right. At a certain point the narrow asphalt roads turned into roads of rock and earth—we'd gone wrong. Had it rained, even the Land Rover might have bogged down.

We were quite alone by then, except for the occasional clutch of women tea pickers in their conical hats, chest-deep among the bushes, hands quick as sparrows pinching off the pale green youngest leaves. The car jolted along in first gear for what seemed hours, but the windows were open and the sun was gentle. A stop for pictures let the uplands' immense stillness settle for a moment.

We were getting closer to Pasirnanka, the plantation, and my mind was moving awfully fast. We turned a corner and were suddenly amidst houses and people—some of them in dark-blue uniforms, gesticulating at us with night sticks! Security guards yelling, What were we doing here? Who were we? They were clearly astonished to see us: we had come in the back way. How had we known the bridge on the main road collapsed yesterday? Renni murmured, "Magic"—and cheerfully set about explaining. Cucu, unperturbed, passed around cigarettes.

Was this Pasirnanka? Yes, it was. Nothing looked familiar, not a house, not the shape of a hill. I wandered away from the car.

My mind was slowing down again. By the guardhouse a road turned left and down towards a large grey metal shed. I could hear a humming that grew louder as I came closer . . . the factory!

If that was the factory, then up that hill had to be the swimming pool. And to the right, beyond those new houses, the home of Mr. Plomp. A tall blond man, he had walked around a whole day with his face as red as a beet because of a telegram from Holland saying his father had died. And from way up his hill, Plomp had looked down—on us!

I started to run, and the group by the car followed. A few steps and there was the Plomp house, a dilapidated bungalow on a little rise, not a hill. And there—our house . . . the garden still the same. On those fieldstone steps my father made Jerry and me promise to look after our mother; the last time we came down them, my mother, Jerry, and I were loaded into the back of a truck with the other white children and mothers. But such a little house! The shape unchanged but picture windows cut into walls, the guesthouse and the servants' quarters gone. The others had caught up. The guards were laughing and calling to someone inside the house. A woman in a pink dress came out; a little boy and a girl followed and clung to her legs. The woman looked a bit apprehensive and didn't speak. One of the guards urged her to invite me in, which she did with her hand. But I said thank you, no—because I knew right then that I had no need to enter, and no curiosity. I took a few pictures, thanked her, and started down the steps, the group following. There were many new homes, but those the whites had lived in were still in use too. The biggest had been Mr. Witte's, the chief administrator's, my father's boss; his house was in even worse shape than the Plomp place.

Every morning, before lunch, all the white families had walked up to the swimming pool. It was the choice spot in the plantation compound: from it you could see all our houses, the soccer field, the factory, the main road. On weekends we brought picnic baskets and spent almost entire days there. My brother and I had few toys, but every day held the certainty of play in the pool. It was never denied. On birthdays we were allowed to jump in with our clothes on. If it rained, my mother said that was all the more reason to go. In bed I planned amazing jumps and tricks for the next day.

Friends and guards in tow, I now marched towards the pool on the hill. At the bottom of the slope there was a tall vine-covered wire fence, broken and flattened in places, the gate hanging open. I knew for certain that there had been no fence there in our time. Inside, high wild grass ran up the hill. I reached the edge of the pool. One rusted handrail still stood upright by the steps leading down; weeds sprouted from the cracked concrete. I wasn't five yet when I dog-paddled its length, eyes wide open beneath the sunlit surface. The guards looked around with interest. The hill top was quiet, shadowy, neglected—where once it had resounded with life. It was like an old cemetery.

Half an hour out of Pasirnanka, on the way back, Cucu drove off the narrow road to let a small packed bus pass us. He cut the motor and lit a cigarette. He had hardly spoken at all on the whole trip. As always, he listened to what others said and responded with his eyes or his smile. But then he turned to me sitting next to him and unexpectedly asked:

"Are you happy now?"

I thought of the place we had just left and that I'd travelled such a way to visit, and I said: "I am, yes"—and realized I was already seeing it again, in my mind's eye, as I'd always seen it, and probably always would. Memory is, finally, all we own.

Ernest Hillen, born in the Netherlands, came to Canada in the years after World War II. A journalist, he wrote for a variety of national magazines, including *Saturday Night, Weekend, The Family Herald, Maclean's,* and *The Financial Post Magazine*. He is perhaps best known for his two memoirs, *The Way of a Boy* (1993) and its sequel, *Small Mercies: A Boy after War* (1997). A previous collection of his journalistic pieces, *A Weekend Memoir*, appeared in 2009.

Joe Fiorito, who contributed the introduction to the present volume, has been a columnist for the *Toronto Star*, the *National Post*, the *Montreal Gazette*, and *The Globe and Mail*, and is the author of several books. He is the recipient of a National Newspaper Award and a Toronto Book Award.

www.ingramcontent.com/pod-product-compliance
Lightning Source LLC
Chambersburg PA
CBHW030205130726
47898CB00012B/888

* 9 7 8 1 7 7 2 4 4 0 8 6 7 *